CW00558640

The Battle Re-Thought

A Symposium on the Battle of Britain

Sponsored jointly by the Royal Air Force Historical Society
and the Royal Air Force Staff College Bracknell

25 June 1990

Joint Editors
Air Commodore Henry Probert
Mr Sebastian Cox

Copyright © 1991 by Royal Air Force Historical Society

First published in the UK in 1991
by Airlife Publishing Ltd.

British Library Cataloguing in Publication Data available

ISBN 1 85310 292 X

All rights reserved. No part of this book may be reproduced
or transmitted in any form or by any means, electronic or
mechanical including photocopying, recording or by any
information storage and retrieval system, without permission
from the Publisher in writing.

Printed by Livesey Ltd., Shrewsbury.

Airlife Publishing Ltd.

101 Longden Road, Shrewsbury SY3 9EB, England.

Contents

Preface

To mark the 50th Anniversary of the Battle of Britain, the RAF Historical Society and the RAF Staff College convened a joint seminar at Bracknell on 25 June 1990. Some 300 people attended, including the Bracknell Directing Staff and students, a visiting party from the West German Fuhrungsakademie in Hamburg, and 150 members of the RAF Historical Society.

Air Chief Marshal Sir Christopher Foxley-Norris, the Chairman of the Battle of Britain Fighter Association, presided over the day's proceedings, and the contributors included the following members of the Association:

> Air Chief Marshal Sir Christopher Foxley-Norris, Air Marshal Sir Denis Crowley-Milling, Air Vice-Marshal H. A. C. Bird-Wilson, Group Captain T. P. Gleave, Group Captain C. B. F. Kingcome, Wing Commander N. P. W. Hancock, Wing Commander A. G. Page, Wing Commander P. L. Parrott, Wing Commander J. A. Thomson, Wing Commander J. R. C. Young, Flight Lieutenant M. E. Croskell.

In addition, a number of historians took part, among them:

> Dr Horst Boog, Mr Sebastian Cox, Professor Michael Foot, Group Captain E. B. Haslam, Mr Cecil James, Group Captain I. Madelin, Air Vice-Marshal R. A. Mason, Dr Vincent Orange, Air Commodore H. A. Probert, Mr Denis Richards, Mr John Terraine, Mr Edward Thomas, Mr Derek Wood.

The morning was devoted to a series of six talks on various aspects of the Battle, and in the afternoon the symposium divided into ten discussion groups in which the issues raised were considered in more detail. These provided an opportunity for Battle of Britain veterans and others to offer their recollections and for historians to comment further on some of the questions and controversies. The day's events were rounded off with an address by Air Chief Marshal Sir Michael Knight.

This volume contains the edited texts of the main talks and a digest of what was said in the discussion groups. Under ordinary circumstances, this record would be published privately by the RAF Historical Society and thus circulated only to members. On this unique occasion, however, it is felt that these proceedings will be of interest to a much wider audience, and the Historical Society is most grateful to Mr Jeremy Gambrill, and Mr Alastair Simpson for agreeing to publish them commercially.

1. Opening Remarks

The Commandant
Air Vice-Marshal A.F.C. Hunter

It is my very pleasant duty to welcome all of you to the Royal Air Force Staff College, and to this symposium which we are delighted to be hosting along with the Royal Air Force Historical Society. Perhaps I may be allowed to say one or two specific words of welcome.

First, there are the historians who have come here to keep us on the right rails; it is a pleasure to see so many of such high calibre gathered here today.

Secondly, we have many who participated in the Battle of Britain, including members of the Battle of Britain Fighter Association — and, if I may mention one name, it is the sole representative of the Luftwaffe, Herr Schlichting, who today may find the arithmetic slightly different from the way it was fifty years ago.

I would also like to welcome our sister staff college, the Führungsakademie from Hamburg, which has a good representation here today. I am delighted that we can continue our exchange and dialogue with them in this symposium.

It would be wrong of me not to say how delighted I am also to see all the members of the Historical Society. Members of my staff and of the present course know the stress that I place on the study of history, and I hope that, after today, many of them will wish to become members, as I am, of this splendid society.

May I now hand over to Sir Christopher Foxley-Norris, who will chair the day's proceedings?

2. Chairman's Introduction

Air Chief Marshal Sir Christopher Foxley-Norris

I was approached nearly a year ago to be asked if I would participate in this particular exercise. It would be linked, they said, to an old exercise, called *See Adler*, which had been brought up to date. As the original author, I will tell you one thing about the exercise which I hope will give you food for thought. I was detached as a member of the Directing Staff to write the big appreciation exercise on the Battle of Britain, and after a week I sought an interview with the Assistant Commandant. I said, "I am awfully sorry, but I have applied all the usual considerations to the exercise — such as factors affecting the attainment of the aim, and the balance of forces — and the Germans must win. What do I do?" He said, "Go and fudge it!". So I did, and it has been fudged ever since.

This brings me to the only other thing that I am going to say in the short time that I have been allotted. We really do want to know not only why we won, but whether we *did* win. So please do not toe the party line when you are studying and reporting on this exercise. If you are merely going to repeat what everybody else has said — and there are twenty-eight new books this year on the subject — it really is rather a waste of time. But if you can think of anything original that might possibly have affected the Battle, for heaven's sake bring it up. I know that I reflect the views of the Commandant and the DS in saying this.

Without further ado, I am going to ask the first speaker to address you. He is the very well-known (and thoroughly justifiably well-known) author Mr Derek Wood, who was the co-author of one of the classic books about the Battle of Britain, *The Narrow Margin*.

3. The Dowding System

Mr Derek Wood

What I would like to do first is to paint a little of the picture behind the system. In the 1930s it was widely accepted that the bomber would always get through, and that's what frightened everybody to death. So the RAF and the British Government decided, on the basis of what they knew, that they had better do the other thing: in other words, create an air defence force capable of stopping daylight raids (not night raids — that came later) or of making them too costly to continue. It was a very, very radical approach.

From 1936 the task of creating these defences was entrusted to Fighter Command and its Commander-in-Chief, Air Chief Marshal Dowding. A lesser man would have been overwhelmed by the task. In 1936 — in 1940, for that matter, — there were no digital or analogue computers (they hadn't been invented), no microchips, no sophisticated communications or detection equipment, no colour television, in fact none of the things that the defence takes for granted in 1990. In those days science-based defence systems were unknown; science was just something that was around the corner, and you found it in universities. It was against this background that Dowding had to build and perfect the world's first operational defence system. Fortunately, he understood the problems, he knew the solutions and he created the system.

He did have certain assets, however. A great deal of research and experimentation had gone on in the late 1920s and early 1930s: pioneering work on reporting and interception, based originally on the London air defence area layout perfected in 1918 by Major-General E. B. Ashmore. He is very often forgotten, but he was the first pioneer. He had gridded maps, he had common counters, he had a method of reporting, and he had sequences and timings. But he also did one other thing: he founded what is now the Royal Observer Corps, so he had two attributes so far as the defence of this country was concerned.

So Dowding had the Observer Corps overland in being, though it was far too small and needed expanding. He also had quite a lot of Army sound locators at his disposal, though I think the best you can say of those is that they were useless. If you picked up a flock of birds, it would drown out anything else, and you couldn't get a direction, and if anybody was walking too heavily outside, that drowned it anyway. A lot of money was spent on that.

One trump card was radar — or, as it was known in those days, radio direction finding, which was the cover name. This was shown to be possible in the Daventry experiment in 1935, and the Bawdsey Research Station had been very rapidly set up. The pace of development on this was absolutely extraordinary when you consider that the British nation is thought always to muddle through and to lose every battle but the last. On this occasion we didn't muddle, we moved very rapidly, very efficiently, and we got it right. Scientists and engineers were brought in at a very early stage, and they worked in complete harmony as part of the total enterprise. By July 1940, after every trial and tribulation, the system had been practised, re-practised, largely debugged, and was ready for the great assault that was coming.

All arms were under Dowding, and this was the key to the system. Unlike the Luftwaffe, which had multiple commands with different forms of aircraft and for different reasons, Fighter Command, Bomber Command and Coastal Command had specific tasks, which meant that their Commanders-in-Chief could devote their whole attention to one section of the defence business. Dowding had Control and Reporting, Anti-Aircraft Command (fully at his disposal after 1939), the Observer Corps (greatly expanded), Balloon Command and the air-raid warning network. This centralization was vital: one command, one purpose. The whole country was on a standard mapping grid (a very major point), so that all information could be understood in any part of the system, however small, and all the plotting procedures were standardized and had been practised day and night until people could do them in their sleep. Fighter Command had an overview of the whole country, being responsible for the strategic direction of the air defences, and Dowding had central intelligence in the shape of an intelligence cell down in the bunker of Bentley Priory with all Service information. Something is going to be said about *Ultra* later on, so I will keep off that subject.

Groups, like No 11, exercised tactical direction under Fighter Command Headquarters from their own operations rooms, and they controlled a variable number of Sectors. The Sectors again had their own operations rooms and were in charge of a variable number of satellite and forward airfields. The Observer Corps, which provided the only plotting and tracking system over land — there was no radar over land — had Group operations rooms (called centres) responsible to the RAF Group they were in, and also provided information to adjoining Sectors.

Let me explain what it was like, and how the system worked. Just look at the progress of a typical raid. It is first seen by a coastal *Chain Home* station forming up over France, and at that stage, while it is gaining altitude and the eagles are wheeling around, nobody knows where it is going, or whether it will split up into a series of small raids or become a main raid. The radar station will give range, position and height, which are transmitted direct to the Bentley Priory filter room. This is vital. (A filter room had been built up in Bawdsey, because in the early days trying to plot and track had become impossible, since everything went in all directions. It resembled a spider's web and you had to clean the place up, marry up the tracks, cancel those that were obviously bogus and straighten out those that were going in a zig-zag.) So you have range, position and height transmitted to the plotter at Bentley Priory. Then the plotter comes back and allocates it a raid number, and that number will follow the raid throughout its career over this country. Once the track has been filtered and looks reasonably clean, it is transferred to the Bentley Priory Operations Room where it can be seen by the Commander-in-Chief or whoever is sitting on the high throne at the time. The track is also simultaneously put down from the filter room to the fighter Groups, which transmit it onward to the Sectors, so all radar information has gone straight up to Bentley Priory and then down through Group and Sector and from there to the Observer Corps.

The Observer Corps has a man called a Sea Plotter; his job is to accept incoming tracks that have been seen by radar. (None of the Sea Plotters was supposed to know anything about RDF or radar, but somehow an awful lot of them did; very funny memos appeared on occasions, making rude remarks about RDF, but the secret was never let out.) The Sea Plotters alert coastal posts in the path of the raid to watch out for it. Once they have seen it, the raid track is then married over the coast and continues to be tracked by the 30,000-odd observers who cover the country. Where (as happened on many occasions) a track is not put up by radar and an aircraft comes in either at low altitude or in mist, those picked up by the Observer Corps are allotted a different number which shows exactly the point of origin and which centre has put it up, and those become raids in their own right.

Once it is clear from the track where this raid is going, or where they think it's going, the Group orders the appropriate Sector or Sectors to scramble squadrons, the aircraft presumably having been put on stand-by already. Once he knows there's trouble brewing, the Sector controller will also plug through to local observer groups, so that he gets a running commentary, literally, on what's coming in on the table and what the observers are actually saying — for example, "fourteen have come down over here, the rest are still up there", and so on. In other words he has a moving picture. It's the age old equivalent of a Recognized Air Picture. The Sector controller now vectors his fighters onto the raid using HF radio. (They all wanted VHF, but deliveries were very slow, and unfortunately there was a minimum of VHF in 1940.) He vectors the unit or units onto the attacking force, giving them any information he can — any change of height or direction — but once the responsible unit commander has sighted the enemy, the controller transfers executive responsibility to him and only recovers it when the units have finished what they are doing and are heading for home.

So we can now imagine the raid has taken place. There have been losses on both sides, squadrons have been airborne, and the airfield they have been operating from has been hit heavily. The controller can get a quick idea from outside what the airfield is like and if it's a complete mess, and there are too many unexploded bombs around, then he will call those fighters back and put them into the satellite or one of the forward airfields if they are clear. Another key part of the system is recovering aircraft. This involves the HF/DF System (high frequency direction finding). Using this, together with the pipsqueak transmitters on the fighters, he can pick them up and, if they cannot find their way home, he can direct them home — very important, particularly if they are out of touch.

Meanwhile we have a damaged airfield, so as soon as anybody can get out and shake themselves down, the casualties are dealt with first, repairs are immediately put in hand, unexploded bombs marked and hopefully either rolled away or de-detonated, craters filled, fires put out. I know that all sounds easy, just a quick little exercise, but in fact it isn't. Even so, these jobs are done in a remarkably short time and most stations are not out of action for very long. Immediately the GPO, the Gas and Electricity Engineers will be called in and they do an incredible job, for which they hardly ever get medals, choked to death with gas, working with high voltage cables, and trying to put all the telephone system together again — and they do it under fire. If the operations room is out of action, then very quickly stand-by operations rooms are brought into use, once the communications have been re-installed. They may be put into a house or a shop in the nearby village; in fact the whole of the observer system has stand-by centres, either in the next house or post office or further down the road, so there is more than a little flexibility in the system, and it can recover from the punches — and does.

When you fight a war the system is only any good if it works on the day, and if you can keep it alive. In addition to the point I have just made about repairs and so on, one vital link was the defence teleprinter network — put in before the war in a massive effort by Standard Telephones and other firms — which literally fed all the Royal Air Force stations throughout the United Kingdom and one or two other headquarters. After serious raids you would find that the DTN was absolutely packed with information; it was burning itself out with it. Loss details, combat reports, ground damage reports, casualties, aircraft and equipment requirements were easily disseminated throughout the whole system. It was one of the key links, and, of course, if there was a raid and the DTN was put out of action, that was one of the things that had to be got back on line as quickly as possible.

In this after-raid period you would come across another piece of the system: the Air Transport Auxiliary, who laughingly used to describe themselves as ancient and tattered airmen — and some of them were. Their job was to prepare the rosters for the delivery of replacement fighters from factory to maintenance units for final fit-out, radio and so on, and from maintenance units to operational squadrons in the field. Very often they landed those aircraft in the middle of an air raid or were shot at, but the supply line was kept open. Theirs was a uniformed civilian organization, and they did a brilliant job.

I mentioned flexibility earlier on, and there is no doubt that the Dowding system was highly flexible. When they had really taken a pasting, the squadrons could be rotated north to rest and could be rebuilt there, in a quiet area, beyond the radius of action of the Me 109s. They also took their ground crews with them (they were flown out in old Harrows or any other aircraft available), so the whole outfit went north. Then, when it came back into action, everybody came south again. This was one of the major differences from the Luftwaffe, which kept the units in place, and just brought in new flying personnel as casualties occurred. The latter was a very good system in some ways, as it kept the experience up, but in other ways it didn't do morale much good because there was nowhere to go; and if you had to go over that nasty, messy piece of water called the English Channel two or three times a day for another three or four weeks, that wasn't very helpful to morale at all.

Another example of flexibility was that, in an emergency, one Sector could control another Sector's aircraft to a limited extent. The maximum number of squadrons one Sector could cope with was six, and, of course, there were range problems, because the transmissions could go so faint as to be inaudible. If somebody hadn't got the crystals right you had problems, but by and large there were no enormous gaps, and one Sector could take over a bit.

On the radar front, we were very vulnerable, with those enormous towers sticking out all round the coast, but (although the RAF didn't know it at the time) they were in fact very, very difficult to bomb. They were only just in the process of building protected sites, and most of the equipment was in huts, which were put under the masts. In fact this was one of the best things that could have happened, because a pilot diving down to attack finds it rather difficult when he suddenly sees a maze of wires in front of him. He tends to veer away, which doesn't do much good for his bombing accuracy. Even so, heavy damage was done to some of the stations. Ventnor on the Isle of Wight was out of action longer than any of them; Poling was very badly hit, and Rye too, but Rye survived. We all talk about mobiles and gap fillers in air forces today, but that's nothing new. Fifty years ago we had the first ever mobiles and gap fillers when Poling was hit, and within a day and a half, I think it was, a mobile was set up and operating in the woods nearby at Angmering. The signal wasn't as strong as from a normal CH station, but it was possible to read from it and to produce plots and tracks. The other point about that was that General Martini's signals intelligence outfit, which was listening on the other side of the Channel, was amazed to hear transmissions coming up again after a short period. Not knowing where they were coming from, they thought the system was still intact. So mobiles were another key element in the system: if you wanted to stay in business you had to be able to put something in the place of damaged equipment.

I think at this point one should also pay an enormous tribute to the WAAF personnel, particularly those in the radar stations. It was very far-sighted of Dowding and Fighter Command to have had WAAFs in those numbers and fully trained; in 1940, when everyone had some hair-raising experiences, they stood it extremely well, certainly as well as the men, and were very cool under fire. This brilliant idea was another of the differences between the Luftwaffe and the Royal Air Force; the Luftwaffe didn't bring women in in any uniformed capacity on an operational basis until later in the war, whereas we had the women from the very beginning, and they were an asset we could not have done without.

One problem area did arise which was the Air Ministry's fault, and a lot of people got killed as a result. I refer to the non-existent air/sea rescue service; the system should have had one but it didn't. The Luftwaffe very sensibly had all their fighters equipped with dinghies, and they had fluoroscene ready to stain the sea. If the pilot had a fire, he would do his best to bale out, and there were seaplanes to pick the crews up. On our side, single-seat fighters didn't even have a dinghy; they certainly didn't have any fluoroscene, and hardly anyone had any training in what to do. There was no co-ordinated command and control of the Channel rescue service either. Any boats that could be got out there were, of course, sent, and slight progress was made when Dowding managed to pinch twelve Lysanders and base them round the coast; at least they could drop dinghies if they could find anybody. Nonetheless, a lot of pilots were killed, either through shock or burns or just being dragged away by their parachutes and drowned, never to be seen again — due to lack of co-ordination. Later in the war, in 1941, we formed the Air Sea Rescue Service, and if anybody came down there was someone on the spot almost before they had landed in the sea. But this didn't happen in 1940, and that is a black mark which the system had to endure right the way through the Battle.

This has been only a very brief glance over an enormous field and a very large system involving tens of thousands of people, quite apart from all the squadrons themselves. It was set up in such a way that it worked and continued to work, which was the key to the Battle of Britain. Dowding understood it because he had been so long with it; he had been in on the beginning of most of its elements and he understood technology. He wasn't a gung-ho commander in any way — that wasn't what was wanted — but he was the man who knew when the system was going wrong and what it needed, and he got it.

I will end with a comment from the other side by General Adolf Galland, the fighter ace. Speaking after the war, he summed up his thoughts on the efficiency of the British system as follows: "From the first the British had an extraordinary advantage, never to be balanced out at any time during the whole war, which was their radar and fighter control network and organization. It was for us a very bitter surprise. We had nothing like it. We could do no other than knock frontally against the outstandingly well organized and resolute direct defence of the British Isles."

4. The Battle of France

Mr John Terraine

Why was it decided that a quick look at the Battle of France —
which began on 10 May 1940 and ended with the French
surrender on 22 June — should be an ingredient of this seminar
on the Battle of Britain?

The answer, I think, can be most readily expressed by reference to the *visual* image of the Battle of Britain, which has been
firmly established by numerous excellent clips of documentary
film, by the vivid recollections of participants who had little doubt
that they were taking part in one of History's greatest dramas,
and by some very fine narratives.

The picture has been firmly drawn: great German bomber
fleets in their orderly formations crossing the Channel under the
unwinking eyes of the *Chain Home* radar stations, with their
escorting fighters above and around them, to encounter Fighter
Command in a very combative frame of mind indeed, and firmly
guided by the Dowding system. It is one of the most impressive
scenes of war of all time.

The key element in it, let me say at once, is the *fighters*. Not
the menacing bombers, pushing along at about 250 mph, whose
mission was nothing less than to knock Britain out of the war
once and for all, but the fighters — by which I mean the
Messerschmitt Bf 109s, the single-engined high-performance
fighters which had made their first operational appearance in
Spain in March 1937. In 1940, flying from bases in the Pas de
Calais, the Me 109s could operate over south-east England for
twenty minutes, providing they did not have to zig-zag too much
in protecting the bombers on the way. Until the Germans had
won the Battle of France, they did not possess bases in the Pas de
Calais. Until then, any attempt at an air attack on Britain would
have been totally different from what we saw from July to

October of 1940. The probability is that undefended bombers would have passed immediately to night operations — which is something to ponder.

The received image of the Battle of France is quite different. The dominant element in this picture is the ten Panzer divisions — 2,574 tanks — which spearheaded the German armies' swift march through Holland, Belgium and northern France. Every day, newspaper readers could see the thick black arrows which showed the German advance plunging across the map towards Paris and towards the Channel. Newsreels provided close-ups of the reality: the grim, businesslike German tanks with their deadly-looking guns and their black crosses, tight-lipped, hard-faced senior officers and cheerful young Nazi crewmen with a lot to be cheerful about. One got also a sense that there were a lot of German aircraft in the sky, but the only ones that really impinged on the public consciousness were the Stukas, the terrifying Junkers 87 dive-bombers.

Stukas and Panzers: the two together, in France, as in Poland in 1939, composed the *Blitzkrieg* — and in 1940 the *Blitzkrieg* was just another name for the invincible military might of Nazi Germany. Certain things escaped notice in the shock and bewilderment of the German onslaught. It is not surprising; the brutal violence and speed of the thing, once properly off the mark, threw just about everyone off balance. One quickly forgot, for instance, that the *Blitzkrieg* as I have just described it was *not* the first manifestation of the battle. The battle opened on 10 May; the *Blitzkrieg* really started on 13 May, when the main body of German armour burst out of the Ardennes and rolled down to the Meuse. The way had been prepared for it.

At this point I think I had better give you an idea of what went before (and above) the German armour, pouring in its dense, vulnerable columns through the narrow passes of what has often been called "the little Switzerland". For the attack in the West in May 1940 the German Air Force deployed the following types and numbers:

1,300 long-range bombers: over half of these were Heinkel 111s, most of the rest being Dornier 17s, with a sprinkling of Junkers 88s;
380 dive bombers: these were the Ju 87s;
350 twin-engined fighters: Messerschmitt 110s;
860 single-engined fighters: Messerschmitt Bf 109Es

300 long-range reconnaissance: Heinkels, Dorniers, Ju 88s

340 short-range reconnaissance: much the same mixture, with some Henschel 123 close-support aircraft and a number of Fieseler 156s (the famous Storch, about which one could sing long psalms of praise and wonder if only there were space);

475 transport aircraft: the renowned Junkers 52s, which had proved their worth in Norway;

45 gliders: if someone can tell me their designation, I shall be grateful; they were about to teach everyone concerned a very striking lesson in the new style of warfare.

The total is 4,050 aircraft. That is an establishment total; the operational figure is somewhat less, but not much, since this was the beginning of a campaign, following a long rest.

In the early hours of 10 May virtually the whole lot was on the move. It was still dark when the bomber crews, without any warning, were hauled out of their beds and, says Alistair Horne, "ordered to attend briefings at fifteen minutes' notice. There was no time even to shave. Shortly before sunrise, every available aircraft left its field."

The German long-range bombers had a full programme that day. The first bombs began to drop at about 4.30 am, European time. The first violence fell mainly on the two neutrals, Holland and Belgium, and it was there that the "new style" was first seen.

The Heinkels and Dorniers ranged out over the North Sea, mine-laying off the Dutch coast; the streets of The Hague were machine-gunned; airfields were attacked, and half the Dutch Air Force (only 125 aircraft) were wiped out on that day. A special feature was the capture of key localities by the use of airborne troops — most of them in uniform, but some disguised (this was when the image of the nuns with tommy-guns hidden in their habits became familiar). The world discovered that, apart from their tactical usefulness, paratroops, when they enjoyed all the advantages of surprise, could produce a moral effect out of all proportion to their numbers. It would be a year before the other side of that picture was revealed.

In Belgium the story was the same — a weak Air Force immediately shattered, an unprepared nation virtually helpless. The sense of helplessness was what counted most, and nothing contributed more to that than the capture of the Belgian Fort Eben Emael (regarded as the 1940 equivalent of Verdun in 1916) in a few hours at a cost of six German dead and fifteen wounded, as a result of an airborne assault in which the gliders were landed "plumb on top of the fort" itself.

May 10 was one long "Shock Horror Mystery Sensation", and, believe me, it did not confine itself to Holland and Belgium. The bombers reached down to the Channel coast; fifty French airfields were attacked; railway centres and road communications were bombed deep into France.

This was of the essence; this was the accompaniment to the whole battle until the British flight and the French surrender. It was this deep bombing which, in the words of John Williams, "wrecked communications, isolated command posts and individual units, and left the various formation headquarters ignorant of what was happening in the forward zones and unable to check information and *exercise any control*". We may add that it also inhibited or actually prevented movement on the ground. By bombing villages and towns on the lines of communication, the German bombers filled the streets with rubble, thus making the quick reinforcement and supply of the front forces impossible. Constantly we hear of the French running out of ammunition — this was why!

And once more there was a moral factor involved — incalculable but evidently of very great importance. Patrick Turnbull, who experienced it and wrote it down in 1978, says:

> *Whatever statistics may be produced, it is safe to say that every soldier, British, French or Belgian, would be as prepared to swear today as close on forty years ago that his every pace was harried by swarming Stukas, Junkers, Heinkels and Dornier "flying pencils", and that from dawn to dusk he witnessed the depressing spectacle of enemy bombers cruising undisturbed in large formations, attacking troops on the move and defensive positions, and destroying every city, town or village for miles around with impunity.*

That was it: "enemy bombers cruising undisturbed in large formations". We are looking at a very remarkable bomber performance (too often disregarded). It was a variation on what, when the pendulum of war swung over, would be called "interdiction", meaning the isolation of a whole battle area to prohibit reinforcement or retreat or supply.

In 1940 it also meant the isolation of separate parts of the battlefield from each other, so that the Battle of France takes on the appearance of a whole complex of separate battles, fought without cohesion and without effective control by any Allied central command — a dreadful picture! How was it done?

To answer that question, we have to ask another: what could have prevented it? It takes no crystal ball or penetrative genius to reply to that: a powerful Allied fighter force could have prevented it, resolutely and correctly handled. The simple, terrible truth of the Battle of France is that the Allies *did not have* a powerful fighter force. The French Air Force had some 790 operational fighters, but that figure only illustrates once more the foolishness of playing games with numbers; "operational" — *en ligne*, in French parlance — only meant that the aircraft was ready and equipped to take off from an airfield. It did *not* mean "modern", i.e. built within the last two years. The standard French fighter (equipping nineteen out of twenty-six combat-ready Groups) was the Morane-Saulnier 406, underpowered and undergunned. There were *never* anything like enough French fighters able to take on the Messerschmitt 109s. No more need be said.

The RAF's direct contribution to Allied air power took two forms. The Advanced Air Striking Force was basically a light bomber force — whose main constituent, the Fairey Battle, was the RAF's outstanding failure of the war — but it also contained a fighter wing of three squadrons equipped with Hawker Hurricanes. There was also the RAF component of the BEF, operating under Army direction, consisting of four long-range reconnaissance squadrons (Bristol Blenheims), five tactical reconnaissance squadrons (Westland Lysanders) and four more Hurricane squadrons. Here, too, lies the answer to the question "what could have prevented it?". For those seven Hurricane squadrons (ultimately to be increased to the equivalent of sixteen) were something special. As I wrote in *The Right of the Line*, "the Hurricane pilots, and they alone of the Allies, had the satisfaction of meeting the enemy with adequate equipment and the ability to use it".

At full establishment, seven squadrons means 112 aircraft; sixteen squadrons means 256. But never, at any time, were the Hurricane squadrons at full establishment — mostly they were at about one-third strength.

So what happened was exactly what one might expect. The German fighters — over 1,200 of them, but, above all, the Me 109s — ruled the sky, and in doing so they achieved, for the first time against a major enemy, *the saturation of a battle area by air power*, and that was what won the Battle of France. It was in fact won in six days. The Panzers reached the Meuse on 13 May; at once the chronic French shortage of anti-tank guns stood revealed. Yet the French possessed 11,000 artillery pieces, and the prestige of their artillery arm was undoubted. But 13 May and the following days witnessed some awful scenes: now was the time of the Stukas, screaming down out of the sky on to the French gun positions, and the unthinkable spectacle was seen of the gunners abandoning their guns. Not just here and there, but along whole divisional sectors; as Alistair Horne says, "there is no doubt that the real collapse began with the gunners". And there is no doubt that the immediate cause of this immediate and lasting demoralization was the Stukas.

What makes that so ironic is that the Stukas were due to have been phased out by the end of 1939 — it was the Polish campaign that reprieved them. And what doubles the irony is their evident vulnerability, both to fighters (as was seen over Britain in August) and to anti-aircraft fire. The latter's effectiveness was amply demonstrated the next day, when the Fairey Battles were shot out of the sky while attempting to bomb the Meuse bridges. The main agent of their destruction was the German light "Flak", the 20mm and 30mm guns; Guy Chapman comments: "the Germans did not waste their fighter pilots' strength in defence, but relied on their excellent anti-aircraft guns". These, too, the French had neglected, like their anti-tank guns, and now they rued the day; it was to be a long time before these two lessons sank in in Britain.

To the accompaniment of a bombing crescendo the climax came on 15 May. It was on that day — at 7.30 am — that the French Prime Minister, Reynaud, told Churchill: "We have been defeated. . . . We have lost the battle". At 11 am Holland surrendered. Rotterdam had been bombed, and the Dutch gave out — and probably believed — that 30,000 people had been killed. We now know that the true figure was under 1,000, though 78,000 had been made homeless; confusion and panic reigned. It reigned also among the thousands of refugees pouring along the roads of Belgium and France, harried by machine-gun fire and bombing all the way. It reigned in the French Ninth Army at Sedan; under the incessant hail of bombs from the Stukas the Ninth Army was breaking up. And all the time the German heavy bombers were hammering at the rear areas; half the French fighter force in the central sector was destroyed on the ground; communications virtually ceased to exist. Panic also seized the French High Command. There was no recovery from this. Reynaud was right; the Allies had lost the battle. They had lost it to the *achievement of complete air superiority* by the German Air Force, enabling the Stukas to perform, the Panzers to roam where they willed; this was an achievement above all of the fighter arm, in particular of the Messerschmitt 109. This was what gave Germany victory in May and June 1940, a victory which transformed the war — all done by the saturation of the battle area by air power, as it would be again in 1944.

5. The Luftwaffe and The Battle of Britain

Dr Horst Boog

(EDITORIAL NOTE: There was time for only a summary of this paper; the full text is reproduced below.)

When the battle for air superiority over England was finally opened by the Luftwaffe on 13 August 1940, more than seven weeks had elapsed since the fall of France. In this period Britain had been able to complete the build-up of her defences, especially her radar-directed fighter defence and reporting system. Meanwhile, on the German side, no coherent air strategy to be used against the British Isles was yet visible. The controversial discussion between the services on the necessity and feasibility of "Operation Sealion" — allegedly the *raison d'être* of Eagle Attack — continued. Joseph Goebbels, Minister for Propaganda, tried to counter the impression that Hitler wanted to bring Britain to her knees by using the Luftwaffe alone. Consideration was given to crushing Great Britain indirectly, either by eliminating her only potential ally on the continent, Soviet Russia, or by wresting Gibraltar and the Suez Canal from her and interrupting the British Empire's life-line to India. In this uncertain situation the air offensive had been improvised, strategically and tactically, against an air defence which had consistently been strengthened and refined over the preceding four years.

The extent of this improvisation can be demonstrated by looking at the way the Luftwaffe prepared for the event. Reichsmarschall Göring showed his lack of interest by taking a long vacation, although as far back as July 1939 his Chief of Intelligence, Oberstleutnant Josef "Beppo" Schmid, had told him of the possible necessity for an occupation of England. And after the victory in France his deputy, Generaloberst Erhard Milch, had proposed the deployment of the entire Luftwaffe along the coasts facing Britain for an immediate invasion of the island. Behind Göring's dilatory attitude lay not only political reasons — he never wanted war with Britain — but also practical ones: the Luftwaffe had lost forty per cent of its aircraft during the campaign in the West and needed time to recover. It was not until 21 July that Göring personally met his senior commanders to discuss the problem of how to gain air superiority over England, the essential prerequisite for an invasion. He gave only some general outlines, remarkable — like the earlier Luftwaffe Staff directive of 16 June — for the great variety of targets to be attacked in addition to achieving the primary objective of gaining air superiority. The British fighters were to be beaten first, so that the bombers could destroy the RAF ground organization later on "under easier conditions", and "large casualties" among the civilian population were to be avoided. Göring did not attempt to co-ordinate activities, and he finally asked the Luftflotte commanders to submit independently plans for the tactics to be pursued in the forthcoming air offensive.

On 30 July Hitler directed Göring to prepare immediately for the "great air battle of the Luftwaffe against England", so that it could begin twelve hours after the date still to be set, which eventually turned out to be 5 August. On 1 August he issued his Fundamental Directive No. 17 for the "Conduct of the Air and Sea War Against England". The war was to be carried on more intensely than before "to produce the necessary conditions for the final reduction of England". With all the means in its power and as quickly as possible, the Luftwaffe was to destroy the Royal Air Force by attacking first of all its flying formations, its ground and supply organizations, and also the aircraft industry, including the factories engaged in the production of anti-aircraft artillery and equipment. After achieving air superiority in terms of time and/or area, the air war was to be continued against harbours (in particular those for the provision of food supplies) and food storage depots further inland; ports and installations needed for subsequent German landing operations were to be spared as far as possible. In addition to all these tasks, Hitler demanded that the Luftwaffe conserve its strength to "take part in full force" in "Operation Sealion", and he forbade terror bombing raids unless he ordered them as reprisal measures. Since good weather would be needed for successful execution of the air offensive, he left its starting date to be decided by the Luftwaffe; eight to fourteen days after that, he would decide whether "Sealion" was to be launched. The deadline was fixed as 15 September.

But the Luftwaffe was not ready yet. On 1 August it informed Generaloberst Alfred Jodl, Chief of the Armed Forces Operations Staff, that, though it was logistically prepared for the big air offensive, Göring had not yet made up his mind about the controversial tactical plans and suggestions of his Luftflotte commanders. The final versions of these were submitted to him the same day.

Fliegerkorps I proposed first to gain air superiority by destroying the aero-engine industry; then to protect the Channel crossing by the ground troops and Navy by attacking the enemy fleet and bomber force and providing close air support to the army; and, thirdly, to strangle Britain by destroying harbours and stocks of provisions and interrupting overseas supplies. Fourthly, indiscriminate bombing as a reprisal might be necessary.

Fliegerkorps II was aware that the Me 109s' short range would prevent them reaching beyond London's northern outskirts. Knowing the importance of the capital to Britain, it proposed to attack military and industrial targets in Greater London, intending also — on the assumption that raids on targets in London would not be left unopposed — to draw in British fighters from bases beyond German fighter range and engage them in a battle of attrition. The bombers were to be used in full force only after the fighter defences had been weakened. A transfer of fighters from Luftflotte 3 to Luftflotte 2 in the Pas de Calais area was already contemplated.

This plan, though less diverse and Utopian than that of Fliegerkorps I, was not accepted because Hitler forbade any attacks in the area of the British capital. Whether he still hoped for a settlement with Britain or, in view of his looming eastern plans, wished to avoid provoking even heavier RAF raids on Berlin and other German cities is open to question. Certainly it was a tactical mistake to omit plans to attack three important fighter airfields and the Hornchurch Sector Station in the London area.

Göring finally adopted a somewhat different air strategy. The British fighters were to be destroyed in the air and on the ground by concentric attacks moving progressively inland, starting for the first five days with targets within a radius of 150 to 100 km south of London. For the next three days they would concentrate on targets between 100 and 50 km from London, and, for the final five days, on the area within 50 km. After this fortnight of assault, it was hoped, the invasion could be launched. On 2 August Göring issued his "Eagle Attack" (Adlerangriff) Directive to Luftflotten 2, 3 and 5. Again it contained rather broad objectives, such as the establishment of air superiority and the reduction of British naval strength, preceded and accompanied by attacks on airfields, ports and factories. On 3 August Luftflotten 2 and 3 were instructed by General Hans Jeschonnek, Chief of the Luftwaffe General Staff, to eliminate British radar stations as a prelude to the intensified air offensive. Now, since three to four days of fine weather were needed to launch the main attack, the opening strike of "Eagle Attack" had to be postponed several times.

The Luftflotte commanders present at the conference with Göring at Karinhall on 6 August must have been surprised to hear him mention the possibility of prematurely breaking off the attack, should the German losses be too high — in which case it would be presented to the outside world as a one-off act of reprisal. This statement may have been connected with the "peace feelers" to Britain which he was putting out at that time through the director of the KLM airline, Albert Plesman, but it certainly also reflected his own doubts about the likely success of the whole operation. At a conference in The Hague on 1 August he had been shocked when Field Marshals Kesselring and Sperrle of Luftflotten 2 and 3 informed him that, jointly, they could not muster more than 700 serviceable bombers at the time. "Is this my Luftwaffe?" he inquired sadly. On the other hand, his self-confidence was bolstered by his Intelligence Chief's under-estimation of British fighter strength — reported to amount to only 400 to 500 aircraft, with monthly production limited to 200 (comparable to German production figures and, in fact, less than half Britain's true monthly production) — and overestimation of the Luftwaffe's capabilities. The intelligence assessment of 16 July was typical of this, rating the Luftwaffe as "clearly superior" to the RAF and still capable of achieving a decisive success. It also predicted that Fighter Command's strength would decline once the intensified air battle had started; the British air-craft repair facilities and radar system were totally disregarded. On 7 August Schmid informed the Luftflotten and Fliegerkorps that the radar system would tie British fighters to their ground stations and prevent swift concentrations at the decisive points of battle; he also predicted its breakdown during mass assaults. The

Director-General for Air Armament, Generaloberst Ernst Udet, succumbed to the same misunderstandings. In a Luftwaffe-RAF comparison of 10 August he praised the qualities of the Me 110 Zerstörer, and the superior offensive armament of German fighters, compared to that of British fighters with "only" eight outboard-mounted machine-guns, and pointed out the better performance of Germany's new DB 601 N high-altitude engines — not yet installed in most of its aircraft. Obviously he did not know that British fighters had recently started using 100-octane fuel, which boosted their performance. The short endurance of the Me 109 single-engine fighter, which together with the long approach across the Channel would substantially curtail its combat time and effectiveness over target, was not mentioned.

These unsubstantiated statements must of course be viewed in the light of the euphoria stemming from the Wehrmacht's first victorious campaigns and the ideological sense of the superiority of the National Socialist "Volksgemeinschaft" over an "individualistic" and "liberalistic" British society that allegedly rested on "profit-making" only. This was a resurrection of the old World War I cliché of "Tradesmen and Warriors", to which the intelligence officers also seem to have succumbed. The fact that men of thirteen nationalities served in Fighter Command, among them many from German-occupied countries, was soon to reveal, however, that most nations preferred a free society.

This euphoria was not by any means shared by all Luftwaffe commanders. One of these was General Wolfgang Martini, head of Luftwaffe signals intelligence, who unfortunately was not directly answerable to the Chief of Staff and did not always tell the General Staff intelligence people what he knew (it was the same with technical intelligence from the Director of Air Armament — there was no co-ordination between these various offices). It was Martini's signal intelligence units that had found out roughly how the British radar system functioned and had informed Luftwaffe commanders late in July of the interception of messages from Sector Controllers ordering British fighters to accept engagements with the Luftwaffe only when necessary, and otherwise to avoid them.

Some commanders were aware that co-operation between bombers and fighters and between the Luftflotten had not yet been sufficiently developed, and that the short range of the Me 109s would determine the range of penetration of the bombers in daylight, leaving many of the fighter airfields and industrial installations farther inland out of reach. But obviously nobody thought of fitting the single-engine fighters with drop-tanks, already successfully tried out in the Spanish Civil War. It was also generally known that the bombers would be vulnerable on account of their inadequate defensive armament. In short, those who could think were aware of the problems posed by using a predominantly tactical air force for an independent strategic air offensive overseas.

There were divided views on the prospects for success in the impending air battle — not least because its strategic nature was not yet clearly visible. After all, it seemed, it was only intended to help the Army get across the Channel. While Luftwaffe General Stapf asserted in the presence of the Army Chief-of-Staff, Generaloberst Franz Halder, that the Luftwaffe was superior and up to its task, and while Göring tried to do the same vis-à-vis his commanders and Hitler, by 8 August the Luftwaffe had not yet started preparations for an invasion. It was still dealing with things in a dilatory fashion by 13 August, obviously doubting the chances of success, although Field Marshal Kesselring deemed invasion imperative because of the short range of his aircraft. The Chief of the Armed Forces Operations Staff believed on the same day that the Luftwaffe would be able to create the conditions necessary for launching "Operation Sealion", but also pointed to other possible ways of beating Britain, amongst them the "continuation of the air offensive up to the annihilation of the economic system of southern England" with the participation of the Italian Air Force. This was not an entirely new thought (the targets selected by the Luftwaffe for its air offensive had always included this objective); establishing air superiority over the invasion area by eliminating Fighter Command, as the most urgent prerequisite for "Sealion", had always been just one of the aims. So, even before the air offensive began, the Luftwaffe had loosened its commitment to the triphibious landing operation, possibly also because it did not want to go on being used as the Army's heavy artillery.

In retrospect, and on the basis of the experience of the major air forces of World War II, the target catalogue was still too diverse, and, when compared with the detailed directives issued by the British Air Staff, too general and lacking detail. This was to render later efforts often futile. Obviously no clear distinction was drawn between airfields belonging to Fighter Command and other Commands. And little was known about the industrial system, its intrinsic interdependence and its bottlenecks, because — except in the pre-war intelligence assessment, "Studie Blau", which had mainly been worked out by civilian experts — targets were now selected by officers untrained in either economics or science. Attempts to use individual expert bomber crews to destroy many targets at the same time showed that the need to employ bombers *en masse* was not understood, and reflected the continental short-war view that war could be decided with the first blow. By contrast, the Western Air Plans of Bomber Command, which in general comprised only one target group each, showed a step-by-step, long-term approach which was lacking in the Luftwaffe, as were any consistent strategic air plans. In fact, Luftwaffe leaders did not yet have a sufficient mental or logical grasp of the problems of an independent strategic bombing war and of gaining air superiority through air-to-air battle, because they had never before prepared or fought such an air war. That it was launched nevertheless was just another piece of "romantic warfare", as Generalmajor Theo Osterkamp, Jagdfliegerführer 2 on the Channel coast, characterized Hitler's and Göring's way of conducting the war.

The forces committed to "Eagle Attack" consisted of Luftflotte 2 in Belgium and northern France, Luftflotte 3 in northwestern France, and Luftflotte 5 in Norway and Denmark. Their overall combat strength was 1,370 twin-engined bombers (Heinkel He 111, Junkers Ju 88 and Dornier Do 17), 406 dive bombers (Junkers Ju 87), 319 twin-engined long-range fighters (Messerschmitt Me 110) and 813 single-engined fighters (Messerschmitt Me 109). Of these, 998 bombers, 316 dive bombers, 261 long-range fighters and 702 single-engined fighters were serviceable: 2,277 combat aircraft in all.

Fighter Command mustered about the same number of operational fighters as the Germans out of an establishment of 1,106. Anti-Aircraft Command had about 1,300 heavy and 700 light guns, as well as just under 3,000 light machine-guns, mainly for airfield defence; Balloon Command assisted with about 2,200 balloons. There were also rockets firing parachute-supported trailing steel wires against low-flying aircraft. Most important, however, were the fifty-two radar stations along the coast from Pembrokeshire to the Shetlands. They provided information on the approximate number and direction of approaching German aircraft over a distance of about 120 km and, together with the low-level radars and the findings of the Observer Corps, enabled the overall situation in the airspace over Britain to be quickly surveyed. Consequently, the commanders and controllers at Fighter Command Headquarters at Stanmore, at the four Group Headquarters and at the Sector Stations were able to react immediately.

In addition, both sides, through their signals intelligence direction-finding, listening and code-breaking services, were usually well informed about the deployment and movements of enemy flying units on either side of the Channel. *Ultra* should, in this respect, not be overrated. From 22 May 1940 onwards, it provided mainly after-battle situation reports, rather than operational orders. Deciphering took time, during which operations had mostly been completed, and German operational orders were usually transmitted by teleprinter or wire telephone. So Dowding probably knew less about imminent operational intentions than about the serviceability and deployment of German flying units. *Ultra* was not *the* decisive element in the battle.

The first days of "Eagle Attack" quickly revealed the Luftwaffe's weaknesses: the inadequate defensive armament of its bombers; the Me 110 escort fighter's lack of speed and manoeuvrability; German fighter pilots' inexperience in escort duties (they were more used to free chase); and the inadequate range of the fighters, and thus their short combat time over target. This last factor also limited the range of the bombers (and the escort fighters, which needed fighter protection themselves) in daylight — particularly in the case of the Ju 87 dive bombers, which were slow and very vulnerable when pulling up after the dive. The number of Me 109s was insufficient, because each bomber, dive bomber and escort fighter unit theoretically needed fighter protection of three times its own strength. The shortcomings of the Luftwaffe became quite evident on "Eagle Day", 13 August, and on 15 August, when Luftflotte 5 launched the first and only attack across the North Sea, suffering high losses. The Germans believed that northern Britain had been depleted of fighters, and were surprised to find this was not true.

In addition, the objective of the raids during the first days of the Battle of Britain — to gain air superiority over the projected invasion area — was not strictly adhered to. Airfields were attacked that had nothing to do with fighter defences, and the existence of factories producing Spitfires and four-engined bombers does not seem to have been sufficiently clear to Luftwaffe intelligence. Finally, the Luftwaffe's awareness of the importance and method of operation of the radar system left much to be desired. Attacks on radar sites were therefore sporadic and soon stopped, because the lattice-work masts could not be destroyed, and it was believed that the sites' operations rooms were located in bomb-proof underground concrete shelters (they were generally in above-ground huts), so that attempts to put them out of operation were soon considered as futile as searching for needles in a haystack. Such views were reinforced when, despite some heavy attacks, the radars continued to operate; the Germans did not realize that their operation was frequently only feigned. Another factor behind their misperception of radar's role was that German doctrine was essentially offensive; radar research had been well advanced before the war, but experiments related to air defence had led nowhere, and the main effort had been concentrated on aspects such as navigational aids. In sum, therefore, too many targets were attacked by day and night, but often not those whose destruction would help to paralyse the fighter defence system.

Göring started to become nervous when the expected result of "Eagle Attack" did not materialize, despite the Luftwaffe's high losses, and the date which Hitler had given the Luftwaffe for achieving air superiority for "Sealion" came and went. But the Luftwaffe believed it had destroyed many more British aircraft than it had lost itself. At a conference with his commanders on 19 August Göring stressed the importance of wearing down the enemy by day and night. He gave the fighters more freedom, though still tying them to their escort duties, and fighter commanders who did not show enough fighting spirit were soon replaced by younger and more daring ones. The Reichsmarschall also mentioned a variety of industrial targets whose destruction had even less to do with the primary objective of defeating Fighter Command, so that the bombers could attack their targets unopposed. He further insisted on pinpoint attacks by highly skilled bomber crews being carried out individually during bad weather and by night, and he still forbade blind bombing. More time passed without result, because unfavourable weather prevented larger German attacks between 19 and 23 August, and the Minister for Propaganda, Joseph Goebbels, began to prepare the German people for the possibility that the war might drag along well into the coming winter.

Meanwhile both sides used the respite for reinforcement and recovery, and the fighters of Luftflotte 3 were shifted to

Luftflotte 2. Then, on 24 August, the phase of intensified attacks on British airfields was initiated. Lasting until 6 September, it seriously weakened the fighter defences, but without wearing them down or causing major withdrawals of fighter units from the forward airfields in southern England. British fighters concentrated on intercepting the German bombers and avoided engagements merely with German fighters. This was especially evident on 29 August, when they broke off combat against 723 single- and twin-engine German fighters, some of which they had erroneously taken for bombers (it became common practice for Spitfires to engage the fighters and Hurricanes to attack the bombers).

So Fighter Command could not be put out of action in the potential invasion area. Meanwhile Luftflotte 3 switched to night bombing and attacked Liverpool four times between 28 and 31 August. Dowding still preferred to rotate his squadrons, rather than transfer fighter units from 12 and 13 Groups south, because he still expected raids by Luftflotte 5. From 19 August to 6 September Fighter Command suffered a total loss of 290 aircraft and 97 pilots, while the Luftwaffe, whose planes and men did not go down over friendly territory when hit, lost 375 aircraft and 678 aircrew.

The thesis that British fighter defences would have broken down had German air attacks on fighter installations been continued for another fourteen days, and that this would have jeopardized the fate of Great Britain, exaggerates the effects of the German bombing attacks and disregards the overall potential available on either side. Fighter Command could have withdrawn its units from airfields in the south-eastern coastal area to bases out of range of German single-engine fighters, or 11 Group's fighters could have been reinforced by those of the other three Groups. And, as already mentioned, fighter production in Britain was more than double that of Germany. The truth is that Fighter Command's major weakness was the shortage of fighter pilots. It had lost about 300 in the Battle of France and was short of about 130 pilots at the beginning of August. Had the ensuing air battle not taken place over British soil, the situation might have become critical. Even so, the deficit grew to 181 pilots from an establishment of 1,558, leaving the actual pilot strength at 1,377 by the end of August; yet by 12 October there was a surplus of 38 fighter pilots over an increased establishment of 1,714. German figures for single-engine fighter pilots, on the other hand, were always about 400 below the actual British strength, with a ratio of fighter aircraft to fighter pilots of only about 1:1; the Luftwaffe had grossly neglected fighter pilot training before the war. Even if twin-engine fighter pilots are included in the total, German fighter pilot figures hardly reached Fighter Command's actual pilot strength. Objectively speaking, Fighter Command's situation was not therefore as dramatic as Churchill painted it, either at the time or later.

Had the Germans gained air superiority over south-east England by 6 September, they could have maintained it only by successfully invading Britain with their ground troops. But this was not to be decided upon by Hitler before 15 September, and, instead of pressing even harder for air superiority until then, the Luftwaffe began to concentrate on bombing targets in London and elsewhere.

Lack of documentary evidence makes it hard to reconstruct the process leading to this decision. Several possible reasons can be discerned. First, as will be remembered, bombing attacks on targets in the London area had been the gist of the plan originating from II Fliegerkorps, which had intended to wear down the British fighters there. They were expected to be drawn to London by bombing attacks on the city, enabling them to be engaged within the range of German single-engine fighters. Another reason for the decision was certainly the belief of Luftwaffe intelligence that Fighter Command had only 150 to 300 fighters left to it in early September, so that the final blow against it could be delivered over London. Colonel Schmid, Chief of Luftwaffe Intelligence, had simply deducted the exaggerated figures of German "kill" claims from the originally assumed British fighter strength, while at the same time underestimating British fighter production. This over-optimistic belief was supported by Field Marshal Kesselring of Luftflotte 2 and, of course, by Göring, though not by Field Marshal Sperrle of Luftflotte 3 nor by Luftwaffe Signals Intelligence, which had provided more appropriate figures for Fighter Command's strength.

No doubt Hitler's anger over Bomber Command's repeated attacks on his own capital also played a part in the decision. These raids had started after some bombs had been inadvertently dropped by the Luftwaffe in the London area on the night of 24/25 August. Churchill, correctly assessing Hitler's probable reaction to bombing attacks on Berlin — he was expected to refuse to lose face before the German people and to retaliate against the British capital — seized the opportunity of this unintended minor attack on London to divert the Luftwaffe from attacking British fighter stations to bombing London, where it could be worn down. He had had a similar idea on 15 May, when he ordered Bomber Command to attack targets east of the Rhine and in the Ruhr, to relieve Luftwaffe pressure on the Allied ground forces in France and slacken the German breakthrough in the West. He thereby started the British strategic bomber offensive against Germany, the longest air operation in World War II.

On 24 August Hitler had again forbidden bombing attacks on London, but on 31 August the Luftwaffe Operations Staff ordered Luftflotten 2 and 3 to prepare a "reprisal" attack on the city. On 4 September Hitler declared in public that he now wanted to "erase" British cities, and on 5 September he gave orders to attack London and other larger cities by day and night. London was to be raided in the afternoon of 7 September. On 14 September, however, Hitler still rejected a suggestion by the Chief of the Luftwaffe General Staff, General Jeschonnek, of bombing residential quarters, so as to cause a mass panic among the civilian population which might eventually lead to the blocking of the main access routes to the potential invasion area. He still preferred attacks on targets of military and economic relevance, although other advisers, too, proposed indiscriminate bombing attacks. But, though terror attacks were not yet intended, the psychological effects of bombing on the civilian population were nevertheless a not unwelcome by-product.

The first intentional bombing raid on London was aimed mainly at the docks. The city was be attacked by Luftflotte 2 by day and under fighter cover, and by Luftflotte 3 at night, until the port, public utility and supply installations and vital sources — whatever these may have been — were destroyed. The Luftwaffe Operations Staff distinguished henceforth between the main air offensive against London and nuisance raids against armament factories and ports elsewhere, which were to be conducted simultaneously. Thirty aircraft and armament factories were selected, and attacks on them had already begun on 4 September. By hitting at the armament industry, rather than the civilian population, it was hoped to hurt influential business circles which might be in a better position to overthrow the Churchill government and establish a new one more likely to sue for peace.

For Fighter Command and its ground organization the diversion of the Luftwaffe to concentrated attacks on London and on aircraft factories was a great relief — although, as mentioned above, it was not so decisive as is commonly believed. The longer distances to the new targets meant a shorter loiter time over target for the German fighters, while giving British fighters more time to intercept both bombers and fighters and better chances to shoot them down. By mid-September the Luftwaffe had still been unable to secure favourable conditions for the launching of "Sealion", but Hitler still hoped it might gain regional air superiority within 10 to 12 days and expected a psychological wearing down of the civilian population by means of the sustained air offensive and the menace of an invasion. Göring believed on 16 September that Fighter Command could be brought to its knees if its past heavy losses were to continue for another four to five days, and in that event would be unable to provide fighter protection for the increased number of targets in England as a whole. On 15 September, while Hitler and Göring were both still hopeful, the Luftwaffe suffered losses almost equal to those of 15 August — the day on which, according to British historiography, the Battle of Britain was decided. On 17 September Hitler postponed "Sealion" until further notice, because the Luftwaffe had fail to gain air superiority and the Navy had expressed its unwillingness to launch the invasion under such conditions.

But, despite its failure, the Luftwaffe was now to play an even more important role. The transition to individual expert (and later mass) night attacks on industrial targets, which were bound to be less accurate than daylight attacks, was expected to intensify the morale effect of the bombing. Above all, an attempt was now being made to wear down the British economy by using the Luftwaffe alone. For this purpose (and also with a view to dividing up the British defences) the number of targets was increased. But this also meant splitting up the gradually diminishing German forces in the air. There was no proper concentration on important targets, since target selection was largely left to the Air Fleets and, as I have said, was considered to be the job of economically and technically untrained officers, rather than civilian experts.

The more obvious the failure of the night air offensive became, the higher the hopes placed on its morale effects, although the targets — except for those of the so-called reprisal raids, which were interspersed — remained more or less of a military or economic nature. It cannot be denied that this bombing offensive gradually deteriorated into indiscriminate air war, though this was not yet intended (as was later confirmed by Basil Collier in *The Defence of the United Kingdom* and by General Arnold in his book *Global Mission*). It was not until the spring of 1942 that the Luftwaffe, on Hitler's orders, decided to conduct intentionally indiscriminate bombing raids. But the resort to reprisal raids on occasion during the winter and spring of 1940/1941 had already marked the transition to terror bombing; the more so since the British did not regard their attacks on German cities as reprisal attacks and did not want to forgo their only instrument for hitting back directly at Germany. Under these conditions the instrument of reprisal lost its meaning and — the more it was used — changed the nature of the air offensive into indiscriminate bombing.

As late as November 1940 the German Foreign Office did not exclude the possibility that the working population of the eastern suburbs of London would rise against the government, as German workers had done in 1918, and thus bring the war to an end. The Luftwaffe Operations Staff had meanwhile become aware that Fighter Command strength had been underestimated by a hundred per cent. On 5 December, Hitler, having postponed "Sealion" until 1941, realized that the British industry and air force could not be destroyed by air attacks. On 18 December he issued his Directive No. 21 "Barbarossa", which turned the Wehrmacht definitely towards the East. England, which could not be defeated directly, was now to be beaten indirectly, by neutralizing her only potential ally on the continent: Soviet Russia. For many reasons, e.g., a more effective British air defence and the fact that the many new and inexperienced German bomber crews could find targets along the coast more easily than those inland, it was now mainly the British ports that were attacked. The air offensive against Britain was also continued in order to deceive the British and the Russians as to Hitler's true intentions. General Jeschonnek, the Luftwaffe's Chief of Staff, was quite happy about the prospect of war against Russia, because he had also realized that the Luftwaffe was designed for a tactical rather than a strategic air war, and that it had won its greatest successes in supporting the ground forces. The prospect of gaining new victories, which had vanished in the strategic air offensive against Britain, now found a new outlet in the forthcoming eastern "campaign". "Endlich ein ordentlicher Krieg!" (At last a proper war to my liking), he is reported to have exclaimed on hearing of Hitler's intention to attack Russia.

For all that the Luftwaffe was diverted away from Britain towards Russia, it lost the air offensive against Britain because it achieved none of its objectives. Regional air superiority over south-eastern England was not gained in time for an invasion, nor could the British war economy be paralysed by the night bomber offensive that followed the cancellation of "Sealion". The diversity of targets attacked right from the beginning of the German air war against the British Isles suggests that the whole air offensive was, from its outset, an attempt to win a war by bombing alone. This was a strategic objective, doomed to failure when attempted by means of a tactical air arm. The attempt was based on exaggerated hopes and lack of experience — as well as, probably, the Luftwaffe's ambition to prove itself as an independent service.

The importance of the German Air Force's failure over Britain rests in the fact that that island could then be used as the base for the Allied air offensive against Germany and for the Allied invasion of the European continent which decided the war. It was fighter strength that decided the Battle of Britain.

6. The British Commanders

Dr Vincent Orange

PART I: THE AIR MINISTRY

My search for the British commanders begins in the Air Ministry. Unfortunately, that institution — which appointed, supported and encouraged those commanders, and also (at times) criticized, undermined and dismissed them — has never yet been subjected to close scrutiny; at least, not in print. Generations of official historians (given, one supposes, adequate access to both written and living sources) have carefully avoided public comment on what Churchill called the "jealousies and cliquism" rampant in "a most cumbersome and ill-working administrative machine".

Archibald Sinclair — its *political* head, as Secretary of State for Air, from 11 May 1940 until the end of the European war — was well liked, but little regarded, by the political establishment. As Stanley Bruce, Australian High Commissioner in London, wrote on 10 June: "While a perfectly nice person, I do not think Sinclair is much good or has any particular force and drive". The Air Ministry's *service* head — Cyril Newall, Chief of the Air Staff since September 1937 — did not appeal to Bruce either, as he recorded after a meeting with Lord Beaverbrook, Minister for Aircraft Production, on 2 July: "We were in complete agreement that Newall had not the fighting weight necessary for the position of CAS". A week later, on the 10th, Bruce raised with Sinclair the question of Newall's competence, about which, he said, he had always had "the gravest doubts". Although Bruce mistrusted Sinclair's assurance that he would make a change, Newall was in fact packed off to a rather less demanding post in New Zealand, but not until after the Battle of Britain had been decided.

According to Bruce, Harold Balfour (Under-Secretary of State for Air) regarded Newall's replacement by Peter Portal in

October 1940 as "a great improvement". He also thought it time
for Hugh Dowding, head of Fighter Command, to go. "This, I
have no doubt," wrote Bruce on 5 November, "arises from
Dowding's incapacity to co-operate with anyone, which has
probably aroused the antagonism of the Air Ministry." But, quite
apart from that antagonism, Dowding's command represented a
recent — and bitterly unwelcome — focus on fighters and
defence, rather than bombers and *offence*, as the RAF's primary
function. When Bruce asked Balfour who should replace
Dowding, Balfour suggested Philip Joubert, Assistant CAS with
a special interest in radar, who would later be appointed for a
second time to head Coastal Command.

There was, however, an even stronger candidate in the Air
Ministry for Dowding's throne: Sholto Douglas (Deputy CAS),
and he would prevail. Moreover, Douglas had in Trafford Leigh-
Mallory (AOC of 12 Group) an ally eager to replace Keith Park,
Dowding's Senior Air Staff Officer at Bentley Priory before the
war and his personal choice as AOC of 11 Group at Uxbridge
during the Battle of Britain. Balfour did his bit to have Dowding
and Park dismissed at the end of the battle. In particular, he
travelled out to Duxford to record opinions on the battle's conduct expressed by a 12 Group pilot (Douglas Bader) which
proved useful in undermining Dowding and Park. Sinclair also
visited Duxford, but neither he nor Balfour felt it desirable to
discover whether Bader's opinions were shared by pilots at any of
the front-line bases in 11 Group. Balfour also received valuable
assistance from a Member of Parliament, Peter Macdonald, the
adjutant of Bader's squadron. "Boozy Mac", as he was known,
busied himself in the House of Commons in support of the tactics
advocated by Bader and, at Balfour's suggestion, saw the Prime
Minister himself.

Hugh Trenchard and John Salmond, the RAF's two most
eminent retired officers, were equally busy. Salmond told
Sinclair, Beaverbrook and Churchill that Dowding must go and
was prepared to appeal to the King himself, if necessary: "as you
and I know," he told Trenchard on 25 September 1940, Dowding
"has not got the qualification of a Commander in the Field, as he
lacks humanity and imagination". Newall should also go, thought
Salmond, because his "strategic judgment is completely at fault".
Trenchard agreed entirely, but preferred more devious methods
of working. "I never mention that you and I are working in agreement on the matter," he told Salmond on 4 October, "as I feel it

is more use our apparently being independent but working for the same cause."

On 14 September Salmond had been appointed chairman of a committee set up to consider the problems of air defence in darkness. This powerful committee, numbering among its members the Air Ministry's most senior officers, brought about Dowding's fall because Fighter Command's inability to tackle night bombers in the closing months of 1940 could be — and was — represented as a personal failure. Rightly or wrongly, commanders have often fallen in the wake of a spectacular disaster and (from a British point of view) the Luftwaffe's assault on Coventry during the night of 14–15 November, after weeks of heavy pounding at London, was undoubtedly that. The notorious enquiry into daytime tactics, held in the Air Ministry on 17 October, had gone far to weaken the standing of Dowding and Park, but it was essentially concerned with a past success that might have been greater; Coventry, in contrast, represented a fearful present and a future that might prove bleaker still. Park had recognized that tactics at night were "those of a cat stalking a mouse rather than a greyhound chasing a hare" and covered the subject shrewdly in a report dated 7 November, which Douglas (no less shrewdly) shelved when it reached the Air Ministry. In theory, it would have been wise to divide the problems of day and night defence, because they required different aircraft, air crews, tactics, ground organization and methods of control. In practice, of course, Douglas would have resisted such a diminution of his inheritance, and Park, the obvious claimant, was at that time bound for exile in darkest Gloucestershire.

PART II: THE QUALITIES OF THE COMMANDERS

Although commanders come in all shapes and sizes, the best of them have certain qualities in common, first of which might be *personality*. This is a quality easy to recognize and hard to define, but if in 1940 Leigh-Mallory had walked past wearing a white coat, he would have been taken for a house-painter, whereas Park would have been taken for a brain-surgeon. It is a quality based on physical carriage (not necessarily personal beauty, though that helps) and on self-confidence (not necessarily based on knowledge or wisdom, though these, too, help). Even German Intelligence Officers, who never met either man, came in 1944 to perceive the difference between them. Park, they thought, had earned the title "Defender of London", whereas Leigh-Mallory was known as "The Flying Sergeant".

A second quality might be *professional knowledge* of every aspect of the job in hand. Park was first employed in Britain's air defence system as early as August 1926 and spent the next six years — some of them under Dowding's command — in posts that required him to study that system. Ideas about air defence, set down on paper in 1926–7, had not changed in principle when war came a dozen years later, and Park always insisted that Fighter Command existed *before* its formal creation in 1936. Not even Dowding's driving force, he thought, could have got it ready in time for the Battle of Britain without the decade of effort before 1936. In July 1938, two years before that battle began, Park became Senior Air Staff Officer at Bentley Priory and privy to all Dowding's hopes and fears for the Command's organization and fighting efficiency. In April 1940, recognizing his fitness for the conduct of battles then imminent, Dowding had him appointed to command the most important of his four Groups.

A third quality might be *the ability to talk and listen*. In this regard, Park surpassed Dowding, although both shared an intense concern for the men under command. They had themselves been through World War I in the front line and experienced that lack of professional knowledge, let alone humane consideration, for which some commanders were notorious. Consequently, Park was diligent at visiting his squadrons, to see for himself what conditions were like at "the sharp end"; he could also explain what was going on in ordinary language and actually listened to what he was told. Both Dowding and Park were receptive to information: not merely to that derived from enemy sources nor even to that available at home, but above all to that which was in conflict with their own opinions or desires. They proved superior in this quality to Hermann Göring, the Luftwaffe's commander, to say nothing of such Air Ministry critics as Douglas, to judge (among many examples) from his performance at a Bentley Priory conference on 7 September 1940.

A fourth quality might be *ruthlessness*. As early as October 1938, Park had told Dowding that Leigh-Mallory "shows a misconception of the basic ideas of fighter defence". Dowding, a less ruthless man than Park where incompetence or disobedience were revealed, had cause and opportunity to get rid of Leigh-

Mallory long before the battle began, but chose instead to hope for improvement. In this he was disappointed, and as late as May 1944 Tedder would speak of educating Leigh-Mallory up to school certificate level. During the Battle, Dowding and Park displayed the allegedly Teutonic virtues, trusting grimly to a meticulously-planned defence and making ruthless demands on the skill and spirit of their men. Göring, in contrast, had the allegedly British virtues: refusing to plan seriously, dabbling with one expedient after another, convinced that the personal appeal — to honour, loyalty or whatever — more than made up for technical or administrative deficiencies.

A fifth quality might be *support*. In Park's case, that of Dowding *above* (to deal with the Air Ministry and with other Commands); that of Douglas Evill, his successor as SASO at Bentley Priory, *on the same level* (to act as a filter between Park, Dowding and other Groups); and that of Sector Commanders and Controllers *below*, not merely to obey, but also to understand and so interpret his orders intelligently. Support, in Park's view, was to be given as well as received. More than a mere obligation, this was a point of honour and consequently he felt it the more keenly when he was let down by certain individuals in the Air Ministry and by Leigh-Mallory.

A sixth quality might be *luck*. I offer three examples. Firstly, in May 1938, the Air Ministry decided to send Park to Palestine and Arthur Harris to Fighter Command as SASO. Park, however, had fallen ill in April and was temporarily unfit for service abroad; Harris was newly married to a wife eager to see the Holy Land; and so a swap was arranged. Had Harris, instead of Park, later gone on from Bentley Priory to command 11 Group, the conduct of fighter defence would have run along different lines. Similarly, the conduct of the British bomber offensive would have been quite different without Harris's masterful direction. Secondly, in November 1939, Dowding asked Park if Duxford should be moved into 11 Group. Park thought the Groups would be better balanced if it stayed in 12 Group and so advised Dowding, who accepted his opinion. Unwittingly, Park had made the most fateful decision of his career, because if Duxford *had* gone into 11 Group, Bader would have been fully involved in front-line fighting and would have had neither opportunity nor inclination to discuss fighter tactics with Leigh-Mallory. Thirdly, Sir Christopher Courtney was injured in a flying accident in June 1939, shortly before he was due to succeed Dowding as head of

Fighter Command. But for that accident, who would now know Dowding's name? In March 1941, when the Air Ministry published an account of the battle, Courtney's performance — good or bad — would have been fulsomely praised, according to the custom of official historians. Unfortunately, Dowding remained in office, and the account therefore suppressed even his name — and that of Park, for good measure. Churchill withered Sinclair for this pettiness, and his feeble response is on record. Eventually, in August 1943, a new edition of the Air Ministry account appeared which actually included photographs, as well as the names, of Dowding and Park.

A seventh quality might be *strategic sense*. Dowding and Park recognized that their task was unusually simple. All they had to do was avoid defeat until bad weather made an invasion impossible in 1940. When good weather returned, at least six months later, the Army should be re-organized and re-equipped, coastal defences should be in place, and the whole air force, not merely Fighter Command, should have become stronger in experience and have benefited from the quantity production of improved or new aircraft and the elimination of types found wanting. But, unlike their Air Ministry critics and subsequent historians, Dowding and Park had to decide there and then what action to take. The Battle of Britain was, in fact, a prolonged campaign in which the challenges posed were varied and unprecedented. It was fought, moreover, by a force that had had little opportunity for realistic combat training in peacetime and had then lost a great many experienced pilots in France; men trained slowly and carefully to handle their modern, high-performance aircraft skilfully. Their replacements were not only as green in battle as they had been, but also much less capable as pilots.

A final, eighth, quality might be *success*. As Churchill once told Portal, "in war you don't have to be nice, you *only* have to be right". If Portal had not come to realize that Park's tactics in the Battle of Britain had been correct, he would not have rescued him from exile in Flying Training Command to send him to so vital a theatre as the Middle East in January 1942. By then Portal had settled into his high office and had had time to observe the actual performance — as opposed to the dramatic proposals — of Fighter Command's new managers, Douglas and Leigh-Mallory.

When assessing the merits of any particular policy, the famous English historian A. J. P. Taylor always asked himself: "What happened next?" I have followed his example in assessing the merits of those commanders who directed the battle in 1940 and those who thereafter seized for themselves the chance to make good their criticisms. In my opinion, if the daytime battle had resumed in the spring of 1941 (as was widely expected), and if Douglas and Leigh-Mallory had remained in charge of Fighter Command, that battle would have been lost.

(EDITORIAL NOTE: There was too little time for Dr Orange to deliver the final section of his paper, but we are able to print it here.)

PART III: WHAT HAPPENED NEXT?

Both Douglas and Leigh-Mallory were enthusiasts for using fighters in large formations: three or more squadrons, working together in a single wing. Such formations were ill-suited to defensive fighting because they took so long to assemble and move into action and were also difficult to control, either from the ground or in the air. Hurricanes and Spitfires had only a short endurance (drop tanks not then being available), and the time spent assembling and climbing at the speed of the slowest aircraft meant that large formations had little time for patrol or combat. Such formations were clearly visible at a great distance and could therefore be easily evaded. Their chances of achieving surprise — one of the fighter pilot's greatest hopes — were negligible. More-over, the Luftwaffe *wanted* Fighter Command to use large formations. In fighter-to-fighter engagements in 1940, the Luft-waffe had enjoyed a distinct advantage; and whenever a great many British fighters were occupied in one place, German bombers had a better chance of an unopposed run to their targets in another. Dowding and Park understood these points, Douglas and Leigh-Mallory did not.

Worse still, Douglas and Leigh-Mallory were quite prepared to permit the Luftwaffe to bomb its targets unopposed (except by ground fire) while fighters were being assembled into big wings. They intended to hit the retreating bombers so hard that they would be reluctant to return. It was a risky policy: Britain would certainly have suffered heavier attack, at least in the initial stages of a renewed campaign, and, given the disadvantages of big wings and the superiority of German fighters and their pilots, it seems likely that the policy of Douglas and Leigh-Mallory would have failed. Ginger Lacey, the most successful British pilot in the battle of 1940, who considered the big wing "a cumbersome and time-wasting" method of getting aircraft to the killing ground, also believed that "if you did not get to the enemy bombers before they bombed, you were only doing half your job". Neither Sinclair nor Balfour sought Lacey's opinions on tactics.

Douglas and Leigh-Mallory, I believe, were incompetent as well as misguided. Douglas, for instance, persisted in the use of Hurricanes as night fighters, even though (as Dowding predicted) they could achieve nothing, except to frighten, injure and some-times kill brave pilots: the pilot's vision was obscured by a long engine cowling, and he was dazzled by exhaust glare, the air-craft's fuel endurance was too limited and it carried no radar. Douglas also used Hampdens as night fighters over Birmingham on 11 December in what even an official historian called an "oddly conceived" experiment. As for Leigh-Mallory, he con-ducted a paper exercise on 29 January 1941, using the circum-stances of an actual attack during the previous September. His intention was to prove correct his opinion on the use of large formations. The exercise was carefully set up, and Leigh-Mallory totally mismanaged it. The raid was not intercepted inbound, and both Kenley and Biggin Hill were "bombed" while their aircraft were still on the ground. When Leigh-Mallory's several mistakes were pointed out to him, he replied that next time he would do better. Luckily, there was no next time, on paper or in fact.

Fighter sweeps across the Channel, sometimes accompanied by bombers, greatly appealed to Douglas and Leigh-Mallory, as devotees of Trenchard's faith in Constant Offensive. The intention, as the famous New Zealand pilot Alan Deere wrote after the war, was the same as the Luftwaffe's in 1940: to entice fighters into the air, where they could be shot down. The British bombers were merely bait, but an unattractive bait because they were too few and too lightly-loaded to threaten seriously any target of importance to the Germans. Their fighters simply waited — out of range — until the whole formation turned for home, and then picked off the stragglers. In 1941, offensive operations across the Channel cost Fighter Command more pilots than were lost in the Battle of Britain. German losses, by contrast, were negligible. The Luftwaffe shot down rather more than four British fighters for every one it lost, and the British claimed rather more than seven German fighters for every one actually destroyed. Fighter Command, in fact, suffered a defeat in offensive operations even more severe than that suffered by the Luftwaffe in 1940. The miscalculation behind an offensive that made no contribution whatever to easing German pressure on the Soviet Union after June 1941 was partly disguised by grossly extravagant estimates of German losses and partly by a no less extravagant emphasis placed on the supposed morale advantage of Constant Offensive. Much was also made of the combat experience gained. It is certainly true that in all warfare, there has never been any substitute for experience gained under fire. But such experience can be bought too dearly or bought in the wrong place at the wrong time. It may be that some of the British pilots lost in 1941 would have been better employed in training (against the day when Russian resistance collapsed, as many feared it would) or in operations in the Mediterranean or Malaya (where the British suffered humiliating defeats in 1941 and 1942).

7. The Intelligence Aspect

Mr Edward Thomas

On a number of occasions in World War II intelligence, mainly
— but not by any means entirely — through the agency of *Ultra*,
helped to shorten battles, save lives, and make a demonstrable
contribution to victory. It would be a fine thing if we intelligence
historians, by showing that there was such a contribution to the
Battle of Britain, could pay a suitable tribute to that great victory.
But, unfortunately, there was no such contribution. Indeed, it is
difficult to prove that intelligence — and I am not talking of the
work of the intelligence officers with the operational units —
helped in any way at all with the conduct of the Battle. I
remember Air Marshal Sir Dermot Boyle saying, *à propos* RAF
recruiting, that the difficulty was to find anyone intelligent
enough to know how to fly — and crazy enough to want to. It was
intelligence of this sort that won the Battle of Britain — and with
little help from institutional intelligence. The most I can do today
is to explode a myth, and to seek your help in solving a mystery.

It must be said that intelligence helped a bit with the prelimi-
naries to the battle. Before the war exploded in the spring of 1940
Whitehall was confident that there could be no invasion of
Britain as long as the RAF and the Royal Navy remained in
being. But after the traumas of Norway and Dunkirk this sensible
qualification was thrown to the winds. The Germans now seemed
capable of anything, and, from the end of May, invasion was
expected daily — and without the necessity of a preliminary air
battle. It was at this point that *Ultra* (that is, the breaking of
enemy high-grade cyphers, in this case the German *Enigma*
machine) made its first contribution to the conduct of the war.
The general-purpose *Enigma* cypher of the Luftwaffe had
been broken regularly since 22 May, albeit with delays that
persisted throughout the battle, and a fortnight later succeeded in

dispersing the invasion panic. Decrypts of signals passing between the Luftwaffe and the German Army revealed, first, that Hitler intended to finish off France before going on to whatever might follow. This furnished an invaluable breathing space. And, secondly, it revealed that, after the renewal of the German offensive on 5 June, French resistance was crumbling too fast to be stopped. This strengthened the Chiefs of Staff — Dowding was not then on the *Ultra* list — to resist French requests for the despatch of further air reinforcements to France.

Three weeks later, after the collapse of France and of Hitler's peace offensive, intelligence gave warning of a Luftwaffe build-up against Britain. The RAF "Y" organization, which monitored the low-grade, tactical WT communications — not the *Enigma* — of the German bomber and recce formations, showed that bombers were being deployed to airfields in northern France where the infant PRU was detecting runway extensions and other preparations for intensive operations. Although transmissions in the Luftwaffe's *Enigma* cypher had declined greatly since the cessation of the land battle, command decisions now having been transferred to inaccessible landlines, a certain amount of front-line administrative traffic continued, and this showed that the bomber squadrons were nearing the end of their post-France refits; also that Fliegerkorps II, now known to be deployed across the Channel, had been ordered to introduce new WT routines from 1 July. This was enough for Air Intelligence in Whitehall to predict that a major offensive was at hand.

But it was not immediately clear whether the offensive would take the form of an invasion or a great air battle. This was not settled until the onset of intensive operations over southern England in mid-July, which enabled the Chiefs of Staff to revert to their original belief that the Germans must suppress the RAF before invading. They had no intelligence to help them. Allegations from Group Captain Winterbotham and others that German intentions became clear through the decryption of directives from Hitler and Göring are utterly without foundation. The most useful support given by intelligence to the RAF at this time was not with the conduct of the battle but with the provision of background information on the Order of Battle, strength, deployment and equipment of the Luftwaffe. The *Enigma* information produced during the fighting in Norway and France was mated with that from low-grade "Y", photo-recce, POW interrogation, captured documents and crashed aircraft, and by the start of the battle it enabled Air Intelligence to scale down its originally greatly exaggerated estimates of Luftwaffe strength. It had put the total first-line strength at 5,000 aircraft with no fewer than 7,000 reserves, whereas the true figures were more like 3,000 and 1,000. In early July these were drastically reduced, in some categories by as much as one third. This enabled the Air Staff, so we are told, "to view the situation much more confidently than a month earlier". But, while Air Intelligence now had the number of Staffel right, they still thought each Staffel's establishment was 12 aircraft instead of 9. So they still exaggerated the number of operational aircraft. What was worse, they had no means of estimating reserves and still continued greatly to exaggerate their number.

So not even the most sophisticated reconstruction of the Luftwaffe Order of Battle was of avail when, in early September — at the most critical stage of the battle — Air Intelligence was asked the supreme question: "Can Fighter Command outlast the Luftwaffe?" Despite Winterbotham's testimony to the contrary, neither the *Enigma* nor any other source could provide a reliable count of enemy losses. AI suspected Fighter Command's claims but had no means of correcting them. But, high as they were, they still were not enough to offset AI's still exaggerated estimate of enemy reserves. Consequently AI predicted that, if the Luftwaffe's losses continued at the August rate, it would be six weeks before its fighter force became ineffective. Coming at a time when it seemed that Fighter Command could last only another three weeks, this opinion must have been most unwelcome. Luckily for AI's prediction — and for all of us — the enemy moved the goalposts.

The big intelligence myth that we must explode is that propagated by Winterbotham and the historian Ronald Lewin that *Enigma* warned Dowding in advance of this German change of direction, as of other significant changes in enemy tactics — and, indeed, of the Luftwaffe's day-to-day intentions. It is true that the *Enigma* gave timely warning of coming raids once or twice in late August and September. But such occasions were too infrequent to be strategically useful. And there were other occasions when signals of intention were decrypted, only to be found too obscure, corrupt or incomplete, or too late to be operationally useful — or even to be worth communicating to Fighter Command. Or else the operations were postponed or cancelled. Warning was given on 13 September that a massive raid on London was intended for 1800 that day, but not that it marked a major switch in German intentions. It failed to materialize; and a further *Enigma* revealed that it had been rescheduled for the 14th. This, too, failed to materialize; and when it finally came on September 15, it did so without warning from the *Enigma*. Similarly, Winterbotham claims that Göring's directive "to wipe the RAF from the sky" was in Dowding's hands, and those of the Prime Minister, "within the hour". This is fantasy. What actually happened was that the *Enigma* came up with one or two obscure references to "Adlertag" between 9 and 13 August, but that nobody at Bletchley or in Whitehall knew what was meant by the term. Then when the climax came on 15 September there was no warning from any source — only from the Observer Corps and the trusty radar. We were flattered to find that Richard Hough and Denis Richards, in their splendid Jubilee History, saw fit to repeat our verdict that "for all his major decisions C-in-C Fighter Command depended on his strategic judgment with no direct assistance from *Enigma*".

We may be sure that, if the *Enigma* had been of the great strategic value claimed by Winterbotham and Lewin, arrangements would have been made for him to have it without delay, as with Gort in France. As it was, Dowding was not made aware of the *Ultra* secret until late October. Such *Enigma* as was of possible usefulness went in disguised form, as was the practice at the time, to one or two indoctrinated members of his staff. But there was another form of signals intelligence that reported regularly to Bentley Priory by direct telephone link; and thereby hangs the mystery I mentioned earlier. The RAF "Y" organization, concerned with monitoring the Luftwaffe's low-grade, tactical, communications, consisted of two branches. One, based at Cheadle in Staffordshire, intercepted, located and, within limitations, decoded — after the low-grade codes were broken at Bletchley — the WT traffic between the enemy bombers and recce aircraft and their controls. The other branch, centred on Kingsdown in Kent, intercepted, translated and reported, to Sector Stations and above, the plain-language RT transmissions of the German fighters. After the war Cheadle claimed to have been able to provide much operationally useful information. They regularly reported convoy sighting reports in the early stages of the battle. They could also identify the bases from which enemy units were operating. They also claim to have reported, on occasion, the imminence of operations from certain of these bases, the identity of bomber units soon after take-off, sometimes the intended target area, and sometimes the bombers' height, course, speed and intended method of attack. The RT organization claims to have been able to detect where aircraft were forming up outside radar range, to tell which radar echoes were bombers and which fighters, to intercept orders specifying main and diversionary targets, to predict rendezvous points between fighters and bombers, and to report routes for the return to France.

We were mystified by these claims. If they have substance, the information must have been useful, especially when radar was temporarily crippled. Why then is it only glancingly mentioned — it was not particularly secret — in the Air Ministry's post-war narratives and official histories? If, as in our history, they are accepted at face value, then insufficient justice has been done to RAF "Y" in the official RAF accounts. On the other hand, the claims may be exaggerated. The reports went by telephone, so it is not possible to trace their impact on any particular day's fighting, and certainly they were irregular and often obscure, and so may not have been able to provide more than an occasional gloss on the infinitely more dependable radar.

On the whole, therefore, the conclusion would seem to be that intelligence, from *Enigma* or any other source, was never more than a bonus as far as the direction of the battle was concerned. It had no impact comparable to that on, say, the Battle of the Atlantic or Mediterranean operations. This may be an unjust conclusion as far as RAF "Y" is concerned, and it would be interesting to hear whether anyone here present has any observations on the subject. Of one thing there is no doubt. That is that Fighter Command owed more to the brains and imagination of men like Watson-Watt and Mitchell than to Turing and the wizards of Bletchley Park — however great their deserts later in the war.

8. August and September 1940

Group Captain Tom Gleave

In May 1940 Hitler, angered by the RAF's bombing of the Ruhr, ordered a crushing air attack on the UK as soon as the Luftwaffe was settled into its new bases and operational once more. The primary target was to be the British aircraft industry. Airfields and reconnaissance of them were added later. We have not the time to examine the "Witches Brew" of orders and directives which followed. However, in mid-July Göring ordered the Commanders of Luftflotten 2, 3 and 5 to prepare plans for an air offensive without delay, and at the end of the month Hitler created panic by demanding the completion of the preparations immediately, so that the attack could be launched within twelve hours' notice. Hard on the heels of this unwelcome prod came the decision to make 5 August "Adlertag" or "Eagle Day". The Luftwaffe decided to devote four days to the subjugation of Fighter Command south of a line from London to Gloucester and four weeks to the defeat of the RAF as a whole. To do all this, Luftflotten 2, 3 and 5 had altogether, on 10 August, over 1,300 serviceable bombers and over 950 serviceable fighters. In the air defence of the UK Dowding had 1,100 serviceable fighters, but only 750 were manned by operationally trained pilots. Moreover, they were spread along the eastern coastline of Scotland, the eastern and southern coastlines of England and round the southern and eastern outskirts of London, and would thus face very heavy odds from Luftwaffe concentrations whenever and wherever the Germans chose to strike.

The Battle of Britain was in essence a battle of attrition. The essential features of successful air defence were: adequate numbers of aircraft, matched up with operationally trained pilots; competent direction and control from the ground, supported by radar and Observer Corps plots; and satisfactory airfield facilities, including good communication with the fighters and with higher authorities and local services. As will be seen from examples which follow, Fighter Command came within an ace of being a loser on all three counts. Because the Sector Station Controllers were the vital links between the fighter pilots and the Operations Rooms at the Groups, the Sector Stations were the key to successful interception. In 11 Group, which bore the brunt of the fighting, the Sector Stations were at Northolt, Tangmere, Kenley, Biggin Hill, Hornchurch, North Weald and Debden, and in the accounts that follow the Sector Stations at Middle Wallop in 10 Group and at Duxford in 12 Group will be mentioned. Other airfields belonged to other commands.

After several postponements "Adlertag" was launched late on 13 August, with attacks on several airfields, only one of which (Middle Wallop) was in Fighter Command. Within 48 hours of "Adlertag" being launched Göring gave orders for Luftflotten 2, 3 and 5 to carry out co-ordinated attacks on the RAF ground installations, and the events of 15 August are of special interest. In the obvious belief that Dowding had concentrated all his squadrons in the south to combat the depredations of the Luftwaffe in the Home Counties and Sussex, Göring set out to give Luftflotte 5, in Norway and Denmark, what he thought would be a clear run in to RAF targets in the north. Soon after midday a force of 100 aircraft was detected approaching the Northumbrian Coast. Consisting of two Gruppen of Heinkels with a Gruppe of Me 110s as escort, it appears to have achieved very little for the loss of fifteen aircraft to 13 Group's fighters. Some time later another force was detected coming in towards the Yorkshire coast. It consisted of 50 Ju 88s from Aalborg in northern Jutland, and its target proved to be the bomber airfield at Driffield. There ten Whitley bombers were destroyed and considerable damage caused, but 12 Group's fighters destroyed eight of the Ju 88s. Luftflotte 5's total losses were twenty-three aircraft out of a force of 150–160 in an operation never to be repeated. In the south, early in the afternoon, a force of escorted Stukas flew over Suffolk and Essex, and a much larger force of escorted bombers covered Kent, attacking airfields not all belonging to Fighter Command. Westwards, over 200 aircraft took part in attacks on Portland and on the airfield at Middle Wallop, while some sixty-plus aircraft reached the southern approaches to London and bombed West Malling airfield (not yet operational) and Croydon, where much damage was done.

Operations on this particular date have been described at length because in several respects 15 August was the greatest day of the Battle. The Luftwaffe flew over 2,000 sorties, its greatest effort in 114 days of fighting, and its total losses came to seventy-five aircraft, its greatest loss in one day of the entire Battle. The widespread points at which the Luftwaffe struck vindicated Dowding's deployment strategy, which must have given Göring a nasty shock. A point not to be overlooked is that, though the enemy bombing of airfields other than those in Fighter Command was damaging to the RAF as a whole, it had no immediate effect on the air defence of the UK and in this respect was a wasted effort on the part of the Luftwaffe.

However, next day (16 August), after twenty-four hours of successful air defence, Dowding and Park were confronted with the stark reality of the attrition 11 Group was facing. As before, the Luftwaffe attacked airfields mostly of other Commands, such as Gosport, Brize Norton and Farnborough, but the Stukas visited Tangmere and devastated the place. The hangars were destroyed and many station buildings hit. The first Beaufighter night fighter and several Hurricanes and Spitfires were also written off. Sadly, many Service and civilian personnel were killed, as always happens in such attacks. Elsewhere Ventnor, already put out of action once (on the 12th) and repaired, was damaged again on the 16th, and a mobile installation at Bembridge filled the gap.

Dowding had lost some ninety pilots, and another fifty had been wounded, some seriously, since 8 August, and he asked the Air Ministry for the experienced pilots of the four Fairey Battle squadrons in Bomber Command to be converted to fighters. The Air Ministry agreed to five pilots from each of the squadrons being allowed to volunteer, and for three pilots from each of the eleven Army Co-operation squadrons to do likewise. This gave Dowding the welcome addition of fifty-three pilots. Some Fleet Air Arm pilots were lent to Fighter Command, and before August dawned two Fleet Air Arm squadrons had joined the fray. Fortunately the threatened fighter aircraft shortage was stopped in its tracks. The reserve of fighter aircraft was low, but not yet dangerously so. The great anxiety now building up in Park's mind was the damage being caused to his airfields, particularly the Sector Stations, and the need for their special protection. The following day Park issued an order that Sector Stations were to be protected with heavy patrols when attacks

threatened. The increasing attention being paid by the Luftwaffe
to aircraft factories was another cause for anxiety.

Events on 18 August repeated the pattern of those on the 15th
and 16th, but it was Kenley's turn to be devastated. Most of its
hangars and several aircraft were destroyed, and the Sector
Operations Room had to be moved to a temporary site in
Caterham — a butcher's shop. Though the Stukas responsible
paid a heavy price for their audacity, sixteen being shot down and
two more crashing on return to base, the devastation of another
Sector Station added to Dowding's and Park's anxieties. The next
day Park ordered his pilots to pay more attention to the enemy's
bomber formations and less to tangling with Me 109s. The "Tally
Ho" procedure was introduced, formation leaders having to give
the "Tally Ho" message as soon as the enemy was sighted, stating
height, course, number of enemy aircraft and approximate
position. It was stressed that the enemy bombers must be
intercepted before they reached their targets. By coincidence,
that same day Göring ordered stronger fighter escorts for
Luftflotte 2's bombers and transferred fighters from Luftflotte 3
for this purpose.

From 20 to 23 August poor weather conditions and consequently reduced air activity came as a welcome relief to Dowding
and Park. On 24 August, however, the Luftwaffe greatly
increased the proportion of fighters to bombers and began a
"Blitz" on RAF airfields in south-east England within range of its
Me 109s which was to continue without let-up until and including
6 September.

To return to 24 August, there were attacks on Manston and
Hornchurch airfields, and serious damage was caused in an
attack on North Weald. Park had called upon Leigh-Mallory of
12 Group to provide cover for the 11 Group airfields north of the
Thames. Only one squadron turned up. Leigh-Mallory had been
attempting to assemble his squadrons as a wing over Duxford but
nothing came of it, and this at a moment of crisis. Use of the Big
Wing, or Balbo, was an unfortunate feature of this period. These
formations could absorb 50–60 aircraft, and taking off, forming
up and climbing to height (20,000 ft) could take 45–48 minutes at
best. An analysis of some ten such formations showed an average
of 56 minutes to reach Sheerness from Duxford. It is also
recorded that, of thirty-two Big Wings launched by 12 Group,
only seven met the enemy, and only once did a Big Wing arrive
first at its intended point of interception. Weather also severely

disrupted the formation of Big Wings, and the appropriation of so many aircraft for a single purpose denied the ability to meet a plurality of other demands. Moreover, multiplication of claims was inevitable with so many aircraft involved, and it gave a distorted measure of success; moreover, such a large formation was also very vulnerable.

The Luftwaffe had operated on most nights during August, and the night of the 24/25 was no exception, but a cardinal error in navigation, causing one of the bombers to drop its load on Central London, started a series of events which were to have an enormous influence on the course of the Battle of Britain, and indeed of the war itself. RAF Bomber Command carried out retaliation raids on Berlin on four of the last seven nights of August and into September.

Meanwhile, during the period from 25 August to 6 September the Luftwaffe attacked a dozen or so airfields in south-east England, not all belonging to Fighter Command, but Biggin Hill (which did) suffered the greatest damage. On 30 August it was bombed day and night, one attack being described as devastating. As a result of a heavy attack next day, two of Biggin Hill's three squadrons were withdrawn to other bases. That day, the 31st, Fighter Command suffered its greatest aircraft loss in any one day of the Battle — a total of thirty-nine. On that day, too, Dowding withdrew the Defiants from daylight fighter operations. The gallant crews had suffered heavy punishment after brief success. Dowding, as a member of the Air Council, had opposed their introduction but failed to stop it.

One of Dowding's many anxieties during this period of greatest strain was the loss of experienced pilots, the replacements for whom were more than often inexperienced, to say the least. So he decided to form three categories of squadrons. The squadrons of 11 Group and those on the immediate flanks, bearing the brunt of the fighting, would be in the "A" Category. A few outside squadrons were to be in the "B" Category and maintained at operational strength and available as squadron reliefs. The remaining squadrons were to be placed in the "C" Category and stripped of their operational pilots for the benefit of the "A" Category squadrons and would devote their energies in the main to training new pilots.

During the fortnight of the Luftwaffe's "Blitz" on the airfields — most particularly the Sector Stations such as Debden, North Weald, Hornchurch, Biggin Hill and Kenley — Fighter Command had lost 286 fighters and about 100 pilots in defending them, among other targets. The Luftwaffe had lost 380 aircraft, and, not surprisingly, only about half of them fighters.

On 7 September a new phase began. The Luftwaffe switched its attacks to London, and this was Hitler's reply to the bombing of Berlin. It was a fatal strategic blunder on Hitler's part and brought tremendous relief to Dowding at a time when things were looking very black. The new offensive was heralded by what has been described as the greatest aerial armada ever seen until then. All told, 348 bombers and 617 fighters took part. Göring, dressed in his pale blue and gold uniform, stood on the cliffs above Calais watching wave after wave of aircraft setting course for England. The first radar blips were seen shortly after 4 pm, and the first sighting by the Observer Corps was made at about 4.15 pm. The enemy formation towered to 23,000 feet on a twenty-mile front. Oil installations at Thameshaven and the London docks were the targets, and big fires were started.

Day and night the raids on London continued whenever the weather was suitable, the day raids meeting stiff opposition. Elsewhere, on the 11 September for example, a Supermarine Spitfire factory was badly damaged, and then poor weather intervened, but on the 13th, when the concentrations of invasion barges and craft were seen to be increasing along the French coast, all Bomber Command's resources were thrown into bombing them day and night.

Meantime the Luftwaffe was preparing for a mass day attack on London. Sunday, 15 September, was the chosen date. It dawned fine and sunny, and at about 11 am a big build-up over the Pas de Calais was detected by radar. The Luftwaffe High Command had laid on over 200 bombers from Luftflotte 2, with heavy escort, in two waves. Another force of seventy bombers from Luftflotte 3 had been despatched to make a diversionary attack on Portland. Churchill chose to visit 11 Group at Uxbridge that morning, and at about 11 am he and Mrs Churchill joined Park in the gallery of the operations room. Park remarked that he did not know what might happen that day. But he very soon did. At 10.50 am Rye radar reported a twenty-plus concentration south-east of Boulogne. Other plots appeared, and Park brought his squadrons to "Readiness" and warned 10 and 12 Groups of what these raids indicated. The enemy formations came straight in, with no feints. Luftflotte 2's main bomber force was met by twenty Spitfires as it crossed the coast near Dungeness just after

11.30 am Park sent up ten squadrons in two-squadron pairs and two single squadrons to harry the German aircraft all the way in from Canterbury. He then committed six more of his own squadrons (one from 10 Group had already joined the fray) and called on 12 Group for support. Shortly before midday Kesselring's main bomber formation was within sight of London when nine squadrons, including five in the Duxford Wing from 12 Group, charged into it and scattered the bombers, which dropped their bombs at random. Two hours later a second wave of Luftflotte 2's bombers approached London and suffered a similar fate at the hands of some twenty-five of Fighter Command's squadrons, as did other minor enemy operations. Fighter Command's claimed score for the day was 180 German aircraft. In truth it was fifty-nine. Fighter Command lost twenty-six. In retrospect, 15 September can be viewed as the nadir of the Luftwaffe's efforts to prepare for the invasion of the UK. On the 17th Hitler postponed the invasion indefinitely, and next day the Germans began to disperse their invasion fleet.

Bad weather restricted air activity until 24 September, when the Luftwaffe launched several moderate raids, and some fighter-bombers were in evidence (a sign of things to come); they damaged the Woolston Spitfire factory at Southampton. The following day Heinkels carried out a destructive raid on the Bristol aircraft factory at Filton, and on the 26th Heinkels from the same Kampfgeschwader attacked the Woolston Spitfire factory again and did considerable damage. The increasing use of fighter-bombers did not go unnoticed, nor the emphasis on aircraft factories, which alerted 10 Group next day.

Events on the 27th proved expensive for the Luftwaffe. Despite massive fighter escorts, fifty-five German aircraft succumbed to the attentions of Dowding's fighters in their attempts to reach London and Filton. The next two days were comparatively quiet but, on 30 September, the last of the massed daylight raids over England took place. An attempt by two waves of bombers to reach London was mostly defeated. About forty Heinkels attacked the Westland aircraft factory at Yeovil but did little damage, and an attempt by fighter-bombers with fighter escort from Luftflotte 3 to reach the Weymouth area was frustrated. Dowding expressed the opinion that the Luftwaffe was no longer willing to accept the high rate of attrition of its bomber force, and could never hope to destroy Fighter Command with its fighter-bombers. The Battle of Britain was virtually over.

Altogether, during August and September the Luftwaffe had lost 1,339, and Fighter Command 723 aircraft. Of pilots and members of aircrew Fighter Command had lost 330.

Victory over the Luftwaffe in the Battle of Britain was the matchless result of dedicated teamwork by the men who flew and fired their guns, the men who kept the fighters battleworthy, and the men and women who tracked and pinpointed the enemy's aircraft, not forgetting the men and women — some in uniform and some civilian — who kept the fighter stations and headquarters alive and in touch with the outside world. That victory also vindicated all that Dowding had fought for and encouraged when a member of the Air Council, and it vindicated the strategy he adopted and implemented so brilliantly as C-in-C Fighter Command. And it confirmed the assessment of Park as a brilliant tactician who, with Dowding, completed a Battle-winning partnership without equal in the annals of air warfare.

9. *Digest of the Group Discussions*

After the formal presentations those attending the seminar divided into ten discussion groups where the various issues raised could be considered in more detail and those who had been involved at the time could give their recollections. Each group was chaired by a member of the College Directing Staff and included at least one officer who had flown in the Battle of Britain, together with one or more historians who had studied the Battle in some depth. The composition of the groups ensured that they all contained a cross-section of those attending, i.e. members of the RAF Historical Society, Bracknell staff and students, and visitors from the Führungsakademie.

As had been expected, the patterns of discussion varied widely, but across the board most aspects of the Battle were covered in one way or another. The proceedings were all recorded and subsequently transcribed, and a small editorial team then compiled a Digest of what seemed to them the most significant contributions. This Digest is reproduced below. It is divided into five main sections, covering the air defence system, the tactics, intelligence, the commanders, and the strategy, with a brief final note on how the original historical research was undertaken. While every effort has been made to ensure that all the statements included are accurately reported, the original transcription was not always easy, and if the occasional error does appear the editorial team can only apologize.

EDITORIAL TEAM:
Mr Edward Bishop
Mr Sebastian Cox
Mr Cecil James
Air Commodore Henry Probert
Mr Tony Richardson
Group Captain Geoffrey Thorburn
Mr Derek Wood

A. THE SYSTEM

In the course of the discussions it was made quite clear that the air defence system of 1940 had not just sprung up in the period from the mid-1930s but had been evolved from World War I onwards. *Denis Richards* responded to *Air Vice Marshal Hunter*'s suggestion that the name Ashmore was important: "Yes, tremendously important. The story does not just begin with Dowding in 1936; it is a continual development from 1916 onwards. It is interrupted for a while when there seems to be no real threat, but as soon as Hitler comes to power there is an obvious threat. It is a sad reflection on us that, despite this continuous effort from 1916 compared with the Luftwaffe's from only 1935, we won the battle by so narrow a margin."

Air Commodore Probert commented that a great number of lessons that had been learnt in World War I were lost in the 1920s when the RAF contracted very rapidly. In the 1920s the emphasis was on survival — the essential concern of the leaders was on preserving the RAF. The threat was perceived as coming from France, and it was to south-east England. Some of the steps taken to meet this supposed threat came in useful in 1940; for instance, most of the airfields were in the right places. Of course in the 1920s and early 1930s only limited resources were available; what we were doing was despite the politicians. Only after 1935 did rearmament become possible — until then the RAF was working on its own without support from the Government or public opinion. The basic belief was that the RAF could not defeat an enemy attacking by day (RAF policy before the invention of radar was deterrent — i.e. counter-bombing); since the Gotha raids on London the belief was that the "bomber would always get through". Then with the advent of the Hurricane and Spitfire and radar in 1937–8, the emphasis switched from deterrence to air defence.

Dr Orange begged the question "Was Dowding the true architect of the Battle of Britain?". He answered it himself: "As Derek Wood said, E.B. Ashmore was the architect. The system he formulated with others was identical in 1918 with that of 1940, apart from the existence of radar. It was instantly forgotten after the Armistice. Air Defence of Great Britain was founded in 1924. Dowding, as Air Member for Supply and Research from 1931 onwards, built on the earlier efforts. Nothing essential started in 1936; rather it was a recovery that started. Dowding was the principal builder rather than the architect."

Air Chief Marshal Sir Kenneth Cross agreed: "I joined my fighter squadron at Hawkinge in 1931. What surprises me is that all the problems that were later solved were right down to Flying Officer level in squadrons. I had to do my time on the concrete spherical mirrors — the first idea of early warning. They were the only protection we had against the French. They showed we were thinking about early warning. We had a Sector Operations room on the station, and we had to do our watches with the Observer Corps. It was Dowding who put it all together, but I agree Ashmore was the original architect."

John Terraine summarized as follows: "I don't like personalizing things *in toto*, but it is fair to say that it would be very difficult to find one, or even two, people who put in more than Dowding in the evolution of the complex system of air defence. The devising of a complex system is obviously attributable to more than one man, but Dowding was the key figure."

Asked how the radar system worked in practice, *Air Vice-Marshal Bird-Wilson* replied: "We went on the order 'Scramble' from the ground controller. We had no effective radar in France. In the Battle of Britain, however, we were told what height the enemy was at, and this information was updated as we proceeded. The ground went quiet at "Tally Ho". *Sir Kenneth Cross* said that much credit was due to the filter room: "CH stations at the beginning of the war were very inaccurate; they could only give ranges. Plots were taken using two such stations. The filter room put this information together, and many exercises were carried out in the earlier months of the war."

AVM Bird-Wilson said that the engineers deserved enormous credit. He described the whole of England as a team, with ground crews working all hours, night and day, ensuring one's aircraft was serviceable, including the radio. Credit was also paid to the Post Office on whose landlines the system depended.

There was discussion on the merits of Dowding's system of rotating squadrons north to recuperate, and putting fresh squadrons in as replacements. The Luftwaffe, on the other hand, chose to keep units continuously in the front line during the Battle and replace aircrew losses in the field. *Dr Orange* commented: "Under the British system we circulated whole squadrons between the front line and elsewhere. In a long war this is best. But in a short war, which was what Hitler intended, there was no need for rotation; it was best to keep young men in the front line. But if it then turned out to be a long war, you would start to run out of your trained best men, and you would also run out of instructors."

Questions were raised about the overall survival capability of the Dowding system. *Air Marshal Sir Kenneth Porter*, who was

Chief Signals Officer at HQ 11 Group during the Battle, talked about the Sector Operations Rooms, most of which were on airfields and largely unprotected: "We weren't worried until the Sector Ops rooms were struck. Only that at Biggin Hill was hit. Kenley had to move to an emergency Ops Room because of the noise from the Ack Ack, and they went to a butcher's shop in Caterham. Biggin was forced to move, and facilities were so poor they could operate only one squadron. Park wanted all Sectors to move to emergency ops rooms — I said he'd lose the war if he did it. I said we could only move to proper accommodation with full facilities. He gave me authority and we did it in three weeks: better facilities than before. Debden moved to a school, Northolt to a big house, Tangmere to an infant school, Hornchurch to a masonic hall in Southend, Biggin to a country club, and Kenley to a big house. The Army and Post Office helped. All were in in just under three weeks. At North Weald they went on using the Ops Room for a while with an UX bomb underneath." *Dr Orange* summed it up: "However battered it was, each part of the system stood the strain; it had the necessary flexibility."

In group 1, *AVM Hunter* asked if the Germans had dealt at all competently with the Dowding system, and if indeed they understood it. *Denis Richards* replied: "The German reaction to the full ramifications of the Dowding system was one of surprise. They certainly weren't surprised that we had radar; after all, they had it themselves. The losses on the initial raids on the German fleet at Wilhelmshaven were so severe that it was obvious our people were picked up. Oh yes, they had radar all right, but what they didn't have, and were surprised to find at the time that we did have, was fighter control from the ground, certainly in a fluid sense. As Dr Boog said earlier, the Germans thought the RAF could control its fighters in a very narrow sense, but could not control them from the ground up to 100 miles away using the HF system of the time. Incidentally we did have some VHF, but it only came in slowly. By the end of the battle, sixteen out of roughly fifty squadrons had VHF, and it made a tremendous difference. One reason why our Sectors could only control up to three squadrons at a time was to enable the speech to be intelligible. The Germans were surprised to hear instructions from controllers still going on when they were meeting our chaps out in the Channel. It was a great shock to them, and Galland, in particular, makes this point. So, whatever they knew about our

Mr Derek Wood signs the visitors' book, supervised by the Commandant.

The Commandant, Air Vice-Marshal 'Sandy' Hunter, with Mr Derek Wood (left) and Mr Edward Thomas.

Air Chief Marshal Sir Kenneth Cross with Air Chief Marshal Sir Christopher Foxley-Norris, Chairman of the Battle of Britain Fighter Association, and Group Captain Tom Gleave.

Group Captain Hamish Mahaddie with Air Marshal Sir Frederick Sowrey, Chairman of the RAF Historical Society, and Air Chief Marshal Sir Michael Knight.

Wing Commander Pat Hancock, Secretary of the Battle of Britain Fighter Association, and Air Marshal Sir Denis Crowley-Milling.

Six Battle of Britain veterans: Wing Commander Jock Thomson (extreme left), Wing Commander Pat Hancock, Air Marshal Sir Denis Crowley-Milling, Air Vice-Marshal 'Birdie' Bird-Wilson, Wing Commander Geoffrey Page, Air Chief Marshal Sir Christopher Foxley-Norris.

Air Chief Marshal Sir David Lee, Air Marshal Sir Denis Crowley-Milling, Air Chief Marshal Sir Kenneth Cross, Air Chief Marshal Sir Denis Smallwood and Air Marshal Sir Kenneth Porter.

Air Commodore Henry Probert, Chairman of the Programmes Committee, with Air Chief Marshal Sir Denis Smallwood and Dr Horst Boog, Chief Historian of the Militärgeschichtliches Forschungsamt in Freiburg.

Dr Boog with a group of staff and students from the Führungsakademie in Hamburg.

Two of the historians: Mr Edward Thomas and Mr John Terraine.

Dr Vincent Orange (right) meets Miss Christina Goulter, another New Zealander, and three Staff College students, including Squadron Leader Gordon Alexander, RNZAF (left).

Mr Denis Richards (centre) with three members of the editorial team: Mr Sebastian Cox, Air Commodore Henry Probert and Mr Edward Bishop.

One of the group discussions.

defence system, they didn't know our fighters could be closely controlled into visual contact from the ground."

Air Chief Marshal Sir Michael Knight added: "It is interesting, in the accounts that I have read, that the Luftwaffe considered close control to be inhibiting, stifling initiative, when it was merely allocating resources appropriately; it is the sort of criticism we have made about the Soviet Air Force in the past. One wonders quite where the balance would have lain, had we ever had to put that into practice. Going back to radar, I entirely agree, from my own reading of it, with what you are saying. Nobody has mentioned that very interesting series of Zeppelin sorties that took place in 1939, which were either totally unsuccessful or wrongly interpreted. They had a bit of trouble with the weather, but we knew they were there, we saw them, and they clearly picked up something but failed to interpret it properly. It's a bit strange really, for we've heard today in the context of Dowding and Göring of British efficiency and decisiveness and, if you like, German romanticism — not normally the impression we have of these two great nations." To which *Denis Richards* replied: "It's not so surprising when you consider we had been thinking about this scheme from World War I onwards. After all, the Luftwaffe only got together as an official body in 1935. They had an awful lot to learn compared with the RAF."

A German guest in Group 6 felt that some Germans *were* aware of the importance of the radar stations, but bombing them was seen as ineffective and wasted effort. The Stukas, he said, were shot from the skies, and there were widely conflicting views on the German side regarding the importance and vulnerability of the CH stations.

B. THE TACTICS

Much discussion was devoted to tactics. Debate ranged from the forgotten lessons of 1914–18 to the Big Wing controversy, demonstrating that half a century later the subject remains capable of arousing rancour and passion — if muted by age and discretion.

There was general consensus that at the outset scant attention had been paid to lessons of the 1914–18 War. *Group Captain Kingcome* said that not much training material was available, though *Air Marshal Sir Frederick Sowrey* urged the value of the

"Look for the Hun in the sun" posters. *Wing Commander Young* cited a series of posters on "How To Stay Alive", dating back to the 1914–18 War.

If fighter pilots were expected to rely to such a large extent on posters, a point introduced by *Group Captain Vallance* was particularly valid. While Fighter Command had developed a highly integrated system to bring its squadrons to battle, "once there, the tactics left a lot to be desired. If we look at the change from the vic to the finger four, we find some squadrons adopting this during the Battle of Britain itself, but Fighter Command operational training units were still using the vic at the start of 1941. There does seem to have been a tactical doctrinal dilemma about which way to go." This contrasted remarkably with the very smooth and efficient operational system of Fighter Command.

Denis Richards conceded that the oft-repeated criticism that British tactics were stereotyped, rigid and changed very slowly, as compared to the early evolution of tactics on the German side, was a fair charge. He said Dowding and the tactical people at Fighter Command deserved to be criticized. "Nearly all the developments occurred in the field, independent of direction from Fighter Command Headquarters." He instanced how Hurricane squadrons had learned in France that "flying about in close vics of three was pretty lethal, with only the front chap seeing who they were attacking". This led to squadrons adopting the German system of either four or two. They also concluded that with guns harmonized at 400 yards they weren't going to do much damage to bombers, so they had to close to 250 yards. *Richards* said Dowding resisted this at Fighter Command for quite a time, but finally came round to it. In no way did he innovate it. Nor was there any useful direction from him on tactics.

Air Vice-Marshal Lyne, who had fought with No 19 Squadron at Dunkirk, reflected on "the totally incompetent threes, rather than pairs or fours" until the tactics changed after the evacuation. *Wing Commander Page* put it this way: "There were certain tactics put forward by Fighter Command, but you soon learned they were wrong. We learned the finger four from the Germans." *Gp Capt Vallance* attributed this lesson to the earlier experience of Boelcke in 1915. *Flight Lieutenant Croskell* of 213 Squadron also condemned the "fallacy of three-formation flying" which was brought home to him on 15 September. "We turned so rapidly to get behind the German aircraft that we completely lost contact.

Suddenly the sky was empty, and I was then hit by four cannon shells from Me 109s."

There was general agreement that the development of tactics owed much to pilot improvisation, *Denis Richards* giving the example of the Poles' predilection for head-on attack, "which was no part of Fighter Command's prescription". The Poles had learned the effectiveness of this tactic in a pre-war exercise. Bomber Command was very angry when the idea was mooted. The question was asked: "Who would do a stupid thing like that?" To which a fighter commander replied, "We will". "And of course," said *Richards*, "they did — a very devastating but a very risky tactic that didn't come from Fighter Command Headquarters."

The unpreparedness of RAF fighter pilots for their 1939–40 role in France was a steady theme. *Squadron Leader McLeod* recalled the early days when fighters, instead of being pitched against bombers (for which, he said, pilots had been trained), encountered fighters and found they needed to "revise tactics hurriedly". *Gp Capt Kingcome* pointed out that training at squadron level had in fact included defence against fighters, but that there was little experience upon which to base it. There was only the guidance of commonsense and knowledge of the comparative characteristics of your own and the enemy's aircraft. He added that 1914–18 tactics could hardly be studied, because there was little visual material, only techniques that were passed on. As it happened, experienced pilots were sometimes vulnerable because of the quality of their airmanship, whereas the crude manoeuvres of the inexperienced saved them.

AVM Lyne took the contradictory view that at least the lesson of the finger-four formation had been learned in 1914–18, though *AVM Bird-Wilson* felt that such lessons had not been well passed on: "We were still using Hendon formations of twelve aircraft." *Dr Orange* made the point that before the 1939–45 War realistic battle tactics could not be practised because of "enormous restrictions", but that from 1938 onwards Park encouraged squadron commanders to show initiative, despite the issue of standard battle plan tactics. These were contained in the Manual of Air Fighting. *Bird-Wilson* preferred to call it the "bible which governed set-piece attacks".

Wing Commander Hancock condemned Fighter Command's "fixed tactics", as used in France. "They were very poor and gave German rear gunners ample opportunity to zero in on you as you all trooped in one after another. German tactics were much better, and we eventually learned from them, but it took a long time." It had not helped that, although he had been trained on bombers, he arrived in France as a fighter pilot. His fighter training was "on the job".

The remainder of the discussion on tactics centred on the Big Wing issue and produced a verbal dogfight between the opinions of *Air Marshal Sir Denis Crowley-Milling*, who had fought in Group Captain Sir Douglas Bader's 242 Squadron in 12 Group, and *Group Captain Gleave*, who had sustained grievous burns before baling out of a 253 Squadron Hurricane in 11 Group.

The personalities and modus operandi of Park and Leigh-Mallory, the 11 and 12 Group commanders, are debated later. The tactical arguments follow here. The core of *Gleave*'s case was that, "time being of the first importance in air defence", the 12 Group Big Wing (a maximum of five squadrons, led by Bader), took too long to get together. He said that 45–48 minutes were needed for the best of them to form up and get to 20,000 feet. Of 32 Big Wings ordered to take off and intercept, only seven got there in time. While a single aircraft was the quickest off the ground, a squadron needed 15–18 minutes to reach 20,000 feet. This put the Big Wing out of it. Even when a Big Wing had time to form up in 1941 to operate over France, it was still disastrous. Supporting *Gleave*, *Wing Commander Thomson* said 12 Group's theory that a large force could knock down more enemy aircraft at a later stage — after it had left the target — did not work in practice. *Flight Lieutenant Croskell* lent further support: "We found that a single squadron tended to break up an enemy attack before the Big Wing arrived." *Derek Wood* also supported *Gleave*, saying there wasn't enough time in 1940. He said Leigh-Mallory believed the important thing was to shoot the enemy down, whereas Park insisted that enemy aircraft should be attacked before they bombed their target.

Wing Commander Page put the time taken to get up as 50–55 minutes, leaving little fuel for fighting. A Big Wing was "just too unwieldy". The time element was not the only argument raised against the Big Wing. *Air Cdre Probert* postulated that, had the Germans realized 12 Group was being used south of the Thames, they might have tried attacks on targets in central England where many of the aircraft factories were.

Sir Denis Crowley-Milling challenged *Gp Capt. Gleave* and his supporters uncompromisingly. He refuted the Big Wing build-up time, which had been put as high as fifty-six minutes. "The moment we took off, and I was Douglas Bader's No 3 on the left, he would be turning onto course straight away and climbing. So quickly in fact that, as he turned, I was always worried that, flying on the inside of the turn, I would hit the ground. I do not know where *Tom Gleave* got his figures from, but it took us about twenty-five minutes to climb to altitude. Bader flew a wing as he flew a squadron. There was no waiting around or forming up involved. Off we went straight away."

Sir Denis suggested that the subject had produced rather more emotion than facts. He went on: "The very first wing operation in 12 Group with three squadrons took place on 7 September. There were no wing operations, as *Gleave* claimed, in August. The operation on 7 September took place after the German switch to London. We operated the Wing only from 7 September to 21 September, and Leigh-Mallory submitted a written report to Dowding on wing operations on 14 September." *Sir Denis* disclosed that Dowding passed it to his SASO with the remark: "I believe that L-M is thinking along the right lines in operating in strength".

Recalling 7 September, *Sir Denis* said: "The operation saw us plunge into a great 'beehive' over the London docks. The advantage of attacking in strength was that you broke the beehive up. I also felt much happier attacking as a squadron than as a section, and, with the Spitfire (No 242 was a Hurricane Squadron) there to take on the high cover, we could do that. As a result, the first thing that happened was that I found myself behind an He 111 right in the middle, and there is no doubt that, the more fighters you can engage with a large formation, the more you can break it up and deal with the bits. In all the Wing operations we did, some twenty or thirty, it never took us longer than six minutes to scramble — two squadrons from Duxford and one from Fowlmere. Occasionally we got off in four minutes. Douglas Bader would take off in a westerly direction and turn straight onto course and start climbing."

C. INTELLIGENCE

Wing Commander Chisnall asked Mr Thomas to explain why Ronald Lewin and F. W. Winterbotham were so wrong about

Ultra. *Edward Thomas* said that Lewin simply followed Winterbotham. The reason Winterbotham produced so many fabrications was that he did not have access to any papers; his book was therefore largely written from memory when he was over seventy years old, and he made up a good deal. Nor did he explain how fragmentary, belated and corrupt the material was, and how much it relied on interpretation. Winterbotham really deserved a much better reputation than he had received through his misrepresentations. He claimed a great deal of credit for himself for the part he played in organizing the exploitation of the *Ultra* material. He wrote that he organized the hut where German Air Force and Army decrypts were processed and communicated to commanders in the field. In fact Bletchley Park's history of the process did not mention Winterbotham once by name, so his claims were gratuitous in that respect.

What he did, and what he should be famous for, was to father the method of high-altitude photographic reconnaissance, which by 1941 had become universally accepted, and which was outstandingly successful as the most important source of intelligence next to *Ultra*, and often exceeded it. Before the war Winterbotham was the liaison officer between the Air Ministry and MI6, and he came into contact with a buccaneering RAF officer, Sydney Cotton. With Winterbotham's support, and it had to be remembered that the Secret Service had very limited funds, and PR was an expensive business, the management of MI6 was persuaded to finance Cotton's experiments in high-level PR before the war. Similarly, the organization for interpretation was also developed by MI6, which developed the technique of the stereoscopic pairs.

The other thing Winterbotham deserved credit for was mating the low-grade SIGINT from Cheadle and Kingsdown with the high-grade *Ultra* from Bletchley. Winterbotham had a great deal to do with setting up a proper organization for collating this information. In particular, he worked on Kingsdown's intercepts of German fighter R/T during the 8th Air Force's daylight raids. This was used in two ways. Firstly, it was collated with other material and passed directly to US fighter squadrons in the air — this was particularly important after the introduction of the P-51 Mustang. Secondly, it was used to reconstruct the techniques and organization of the German defences on both day and night raids — the areas of German strength, deployments, etc. This was definitely best done by fusing low- and high-grade SIGINT.

Winterbotham brought that about and those were his real triumphs.

Edward Thomas then expanded on the "Y" service. He had hoped that there might have been people present who had some direct experience of the impact of low-grade SIGINT. The historian was confronted with claims from West Kingsdown and Cheadle that they produced information which should have been extremely useful, especially when the radar warning system was crippled from time to time. Cheadle monitored morse and other traffic and took D/F bearings, as well as decoding the air/ground traffic and identifying call-signs, and claimed to be able to identify the bases from which enemy units were operating; the imminence of operations from those bases; the identity of bomber units soon after take-off; the intended target areas, deduced from the pattern of medium-frequency navigation-beacon transmissions; and the height, course, speed and intended method of attack of the bombers (the latter sometimes used R/T for station-keeping purposes). West Kingsdown claimed to be able to detect where aircraft were forming up beyond radar range (not invariably, but sometimes), and which radar plots were bombers and which were fighters; to intercept orders specifying main and diversionary targets; to predict rendezvous points between bombers and fighters; and to predict return routes to France. On the face of it that was valuable information. To what extent it would have been received at the operations rooms at Sector stations, Groups and Fighter Command in time to influence a battle which was whirling overhead one doesn't know. All the people at Cheadle and Kingsdown knew was that they supplied the information, but that could be a long way from its being useful.

Group Captain Haslam recalled talking to Aileen Clayton, who was the first woman intelligence officer, and a fine German speaker, and she could identify which German pilot it was. But he was unaware what effect that had on the Battle, even transmitted directly to Fighter Command. *Edward Thomas* said he thought in her book (*The Enemy is Listening*) Mrs Clayton tended to emphasize the human side, which did not tell the historian very much. Nor did she see the whole story, and there was an awful lot of hearsay in her account — so, all in all, he was somewhat critical of it. But these claims were made, and, oddly enough, the only person who had told him of an instance where the information was useful was *Professor M. R. D. Foot* after the lecture that morning.

Professor Foot related that he had been an anti-aircraft liaison officer at Hornchurch and could remember the plot at Hornchurch telling him that they were expecting a raid to come in from a certain direction long before there were any indications from radar, and that this happened more than once. No such contribution had been recorded or acknowledged, but there seemed to be strong evidence of intelligence derived from "Y", for example in identifying and quantifying raids as aircraft assembled over the area between Calais and Lille. *Edward Thomas* commented that Professor Foot's recollections agreed with the claims that they could identify the bases and could sometimes tell if operations were imminent from them because, half an hour before take-off, the bombers would calibrate their frequencies — which were of course changed daily, necessitating retuning the crystals. Those test transmissions were intercepted. *Thomas* would have thought this was useful — *Foot* said it helped them alert the radar to the direction of a raid. That was, however, the first time *Thomas* had heard anybody say that it was of any use. There was nothing about it in the RAF narratives, yet this was low-grade material, passed over the telephone quite openly and, from the extravagant claims made after the war, it should have been quite useful at the time.

Cecil James accepted that no such evidence was available to the Air Historical Branch during the war, when knowledge of the existing "Y" service was very closely confined. The documented plots of attacks as they assembled were assumed to be based on radar intelligence. *Group Captain Verity* said that, though he was not involved in the battle, he later became very aware of the valuable influence of "Y" service information and felt that its significance during the Battle might have been understated during *Edward Thomas'* lecture.

Air Vice-Marshal Black questioned the value of knowing where exactly an attack came from. Without wishing to decry intelligence, the important thing was the rate of attrition inflicted on the attackers. *Edward Thomas* responded that he was there to decry it. When the Official Historians had been asked to write the history of British intelligence, they were given three years and were expected to write up one or two outstanding successes, but instead they found that there was another side to the coin and duly recorded it. Instead of taking three years it took twenty, but the entire history was there, warts and all. He suspected that this was a case where, although the claims made for "Y" after the war were quite extravagant, in fact it could not have made a very great impact. So, with the low-grade making no impact, and the *Ultra* making no impact, there was not much else to make one!

Derek Wood expressed the view that the "Y" service at Kingsdown was formed almost by accident, when Group Captain Scott Farnie bought his own receivers. The "Y" service were able to establish the position of enemy formations, but the information was not always passed on because of a lack of communications. *Air Chief Marshal Sir Denis Smallwood* commented that in his experience, although the "Y" service was sometimes inaccurate, it was generally invaluable.

Wing Commander Hancock revealed that, once the German offensive in France opened on 10 May 1940, the first thing that happened was that the carefully laid mobile radar network that had been established near the German frontier was destroyed, and the RAF reverted to a pre-war patrol system. His squadron was the recipient of one piece of good intelligence, when they were told that the Germans were coming to attack some troops at St-Valéry-en-Caux. The intelligence was accurate, because 150 German aircraft duly appeared. He had never seen more than the odd one until that time, so it was certainly an eye-opener, especially as they shot him up!

Elsewhere German intelligence was discussed, and *Sebastian Cox* said that its failings were widespread and fundamental. In a famous assessment of 16 July 1940, "Beppo" Schmid, Head of Luftwaffe Intelligence, failed to mention British radar at all and characterized the British system as inflexible, when precisely the opposite was true. In fact, Schmid had identified every British strength as a weakness, and every weakness as a strength. He had, for example, predicted that the RAF would not suffer any pilot shortage, stated that British aircraft production was inferior to Germany's, and painted the RAF leadership as out of touch. On every count he was in error, and with that intelligence background it became very difficult for the German High Command to make any sensible command decisions. Partly as a result of this, the Germans failed to adopt a settled strategy. In other words, they had transgressed a fundamental principle of war — the maintenance of the aim. Once they decided to attack London, the erroneous assessments from Luftwaffe intelligence had a crucial effect. At least some of the senior German commanders believed that Fighter Command had only some 150 fighters remaining, and that by attacking London these could be drawn into a climactic battle over the capital. However, the actual result was to relieve the pressure on Dowding's severely battered system and thus allow Fighter Command to recover its balance. It was also easier for the defence to track incoming raids, and easier for Fighter Command to deploy the strength of 12 Group from north of the Thames. At the same time, the Luftwaffe compounded its own problems because it penetrated deeper into British territory, increasing its own losses, and reducing the effectiveness of the Me 109s. The major factors behind German command mistakes were overconfidence, engendered by their early victories in Europe, and poor intelligence, stemming in large part from organizational failures.

Derek Wood, responding to a question about the poor quality of the Luftwaffe's target intelligence, said that in the immediate pre-war period Lufthansa aircraft had conducted clandestine photographic reconnaissance over British airfields. The Luftwaffe had also acquired a full set of British ordnance survey maps: Field Marshal Milch had subsequently told him that they had been ordered by post! During June and July many single aircraft, mostly Dornier 17s, had also conducted PR sorties, and some recce aircraft were sent over to conduct post-raid reconnaissance. However, "Beppo" Schmid had very little appreciation of PR, and in consequence the Luftwaffe bombed *all* airfields, and not just those allocated to Fighter Command.

Herr Schlichting, a Ju 88 reconnaissance pilot, described his operations over the UK from the summer of 1940 into 1943 — during which time he was only once intercepted (over Bristol) and succeeded in returning to France, despite the damage to his aircraft. He believed that about seventy per cent of the UK had been photographed. When operations by day became too hazardous, sorties were flown at night at 12,000 feet, and photos were taken by the light of flares. He attributed his survival partly to the performance of the Ju 88, which was only marginally inferior to British night fighters, and to effective radar warning equipment. Nevertheless, many of his staff were lost on these operations. As time went on, his reconnaissance task was moved westwards, including the Western Approaches.

Wing Commander Romsey asked whether the poor assessments of German intelligence stemmed from deliberate British deception measures. *Sebastian Cox* thought not. Rather, German intelligence failings were the result, largely, of the bureaucratic structures of the Third Reich. Hitler had created, quite deliberately, a vertical society in which information flowed upwards to the Führer. There was little horizontal dissemination, so that, for example, Martini's radio intelligence service knew about radar and the R/T system, but much of that knowledge, and with it power, was not willingly surrendered to rivals within the system. The British, of course, had their own bureaucratic infighting, but it was not systemic in the same way. In Germany you would never have found a POW interrogation report on a new type of tracer ammunition being distributed to some 40 individuals, including the Director of Armament Development at the Ministry of Aircraft Production, as happened in Britain.

D. THE COMMANDERS

Much time was devoted to the merits of, and differences between, the senior commanders, most of the contributions coming from the historians. As *Sir Christopher Foxley-Norris* said, reflecting the views of the majority of the other Battle participants: "You will all find when you get to be Air Chief Marshals that people think you have always been an Air Chief Marshal and say 'What did you think of Dowding'; if you saw a Group Captain in 1940 you went and hid behind a hut. I knew nothing of Dowding, except that I nearly killed him by knocking a cricket ball over his head on the field just outside here. The average pilot was lucky if he knew the station commander."

Denis Richards commented at length on the subject, beginning with the relationship between the Air Ministry and Commanders-in-Chief: "The commander in the field has a responsibility only to his command, and he tends to view that, particularly if he is a good commander, absolutely wholeheartedly. The result is that anyone who doesn't give him everything that he wants is a bit of a villain. So the Air Ministry appears like that not only to Dowding, because he didn't get enough fighters, but also to Harris, because he didn't get enough bombers, and to Slessor, because he didn't get enough Coastal aircraft. They are all seen as boneheads at the Air Ministry, and yet these officers themselves were the Air Ministry a few years before. Indeed, if their ambitions were to be realized and they became CAS, they would become Air Ministry again. They would not have changed their intelligence or their characters on transition from one place to another. It is all too easy just to snipe at the set of so-called boneheads in the War Office, the Air Ministry or the Admiralty."

Sebastian Cox echoed this view: "You may have garnered an impression from this morning's proceedings that everybody in the Air Ministry was either a knave or a fool. I do not believe that they were. Portal most certainly was not, and neither was his Vice-Chief, Freeman."

Group Captain Haslam pursued a similar theme: "I disagreed with Vincent Orange when he quoted the Australian High Commissioner on British Ministers — it did not seem to me a good historical source. For example, Sinclair was Churchill's second-in-command in the trenches in France in 1916. He was absolutely straight, a true gentleman, and by no means a negligible personality. With regard to Newall, he was CAS when we were developing Fighter Command, and he likewise was not a negligible character, and it was Newall who confronted the Cabinet and said 'no more aircraft to France'."

The main discussion, however, concentrated on Dowding, Park and Leigh-Mallory, and there was considerable disagreement arising from *Dr Orange's* earlier statements. In Orange's own group *AVM Bird-Wilson* commented: "I was nineteen at the time. From hindsight we always knock our leaders. I put Dowding as the strategic planner — we should have got nothing in the organization without him. Park was a superb tactical commander; he led from the front. Returning from Dunkirk we had to land at Manston, and Park walked into the Mess, having just come back from Dunkirk himself. We never saw Dowding or Leigh-Mallory. Barratt we did see, and he talked about every other squadron but ours."

Sir Kenneth Cross, however, took *Dr Orange* to task: "You were a little unkind to Leigh-Mallory. Park took over 11 Group in early 1940, as a ready-made organization, but Leigh-Mallory took over 12 Group from nothing and built it up, together with 13 Group. I served on his staff for a year, and how he worked. He felt that he knew the overall system better than Park."

Dr Orange then commented: "Dowding, behind his gruff exterior, was not in fact gruff and difficult — he was an old softie, once you got through to him. Park, on the other hand, could be a very hard man when it came to firing people. But Dowding did not get rid of people. In 1938–40 Dowding and Park often corresponded on the files, with Park, the young Air Commodore, continually pressing Dowding to do something about Leigh-

Mallory and others. But Dowding saw himself as head of the family, wanting to educate Leigh-Mallory into seeing the light. I think he should have removed him. He had the opportunities but did not take them, for he was too kind-hearted."

Several of the Battle of Britain pilots expressed their views on these issues, including *Wg Cdr Hancock*: "We were only junior officers in the Battle of Britain, but we thought Park was splendid, and the views on Leigh-Mallory which percolated down led us to believe there was no smoke without fire. I had the misfortune to meet Leigh-Mallory on one occasion, and the way he harangued the pilots of 266 before we went to France, that is during the 'Phoney War', was most unpleasant, particularly as there was no reason for it. We have all torn strips off people, and had it done to us, deservedly so, but to be told by your AOC that you are all useless for no good reason at all; well, we went off him."

Another was *Gp Capt Kingcome*, who agreed that Park (well known as an active pilot and regular visitor) and Dowding were the architects of the victory. Dowding, though not universally popular, was a man of total loyalty and integrity who did not suffer fools; he was not a promotion or impression seeker but was intent on getting the job done. Leigh-Mallory was not of the same calibre, and had he occupied either of the other two positions serious problems would have resulted. Keen to get into the action he used Bader's Big Wing concept to do so — Bader had integrity, drive and guts, but was an egotist who felt out of things.

This subject was further explored when *Sir Kenneth Porter* gave his recollections: "I was at HQ 11 Group but used to visit Bentley Priory. The real architect was Park, who had been SASO at Fighter Command, which helped make him such a good commander of 11 Group. Leigh-Mallory did not understand the system at all. At the time Park went to 11 Group this was not, of course, the important one, and he was very junior, only an Acting AVM. Leigh-Mallory, as a senior AVM, had thought of himself as the important man, and then found he wasn't — Park, as the junior, was getting all the battle, and Leigh-Mallory wanted to be in on it. He only started to become jealous after the battle started, when he was being asked mainly to provide the reinforcements. He then started listening to Bader. Originally, Park was amenable to requesting Leigh-Mallory's help, but Duxford squadrons could only be controlled from the ground as far as the Thames, not further south. Thereafter they were out of control, and the Observer Corps was reporting them as enemy raids. Park was right to complain, because it was not paying the dividends it should have done.

"I served with both Park and Leigh-Mallory. At first I thought Leigh-Mallory was useless, but he learnt very quickly. He later ran a paper exercise in the Ops Room which failed, and this converted him against the Big Wing. He didn't, however, make decisions as quickly as Park. Park's conduct of the Battle of Britain was brilliant; he held a morning meeting, and then flew around the airfields, talking to the pilots. Decisions were made by telephone (nobody used a file), and everything was done quickly. Everybody admired him, but he was a most unlovable man. Leigh-Mallory, on the other hand, was a very nice man, but he relied heavily on advice. Bader impressed him, and he took his advice on the Big Wing. Then at 11 Group he took advice elsewhere, and always he picked people he thought knew what they were talking about and used them. Park never did this, and he made enemies. He had no friends in the hierarchy; he was a loner. Leigh-Mallory was much senior and got on well with other people, including the Americans. He was not as pompous as some thought."

Gp Capt. Gleave immediately commented: "Park was worshipped on the squadrons — he was a real fighting AOC, and it was important for the pilots to have an AOC they could admire. And Leigh-Mallory *was* pompous."

Some of their views were echoed in group 6, where *Wg Cdr Thomson* said that the rivalry between Park and Leigh-Mallory was well known, with letters on the subject surprisingly being circulated down to squadron level; the argument was seen as childish. *Thomson* admired Park, recalling that he had flown over the Dunkirk beaches and then arrived to speak to the pilots at Hawkinge, who had been operating over Dunkirk. This was very good for morale and showed that Park was at the sharp end. Unlike Leigh-Mallory, Park was a pilot's man — you felt you were talking to a fellow tradesman. As for Dowding, *Thomson* said that the pilots knew he existed but rarely saw him; however, they much resented his removal and the denial of recognition, i.e. the failure to make him a Marshal of the RAF.

AVM Lyne, who had flown with 19 Squadron at Dunkirk, also offered some personal recollections, having met Park later in the war, in the Far East. Here Park had devoted much time to telling him and his colleagues how good his command was but had never asked them as informed visitors for their views. He had seemed vain and opinionated, not a listener. By contrast, Tedder used to visit his desert squadrons and sit at the back of the tent listening; it was wonderful to think that he was there and knew what the chaps thought. *Lyne* went on to point out that in World War II the older generation surrendered command to the youngsters; in the Battle of Britain the Group Captains stayed out of the front line, deferring to the younger men. In this setting Leigh-Mallory appeared insecure and hesitant, and the influence of Bader, who was older than most, was not surprising.

Air Chief Marshal Sir John Aiken, who met Dowding twice after the war, accepted that all his pilots spoke highly of him. But he had found Dowding cold and unimpressive, though courteous; he was not a commanding figure, not what one would have expected of a great commander. The rivalry between Park and Leigh-Mallory was dangerous, and Dowding should have taken a firm stand and intervened. "I saw Leigh-Mallory; he stalked round the dispersal and would not talk directly to pilots. We were lucky that Park was there."

Air Cdre Probert reminded the group that Leigh-Mallory's task during the Battle was to defend the East Coast and Midlands (just as Saul in 13 Group had to defend the North-East), to provide reinforcements, and to help defend Park's airfields, so he was limited in what he could do. Being senior to Park, he felt aggrieved at not having been given 11 Group, and his pilots, too, understandably wanted a share of the action. Dowding should have rotated his squadrons more — he could, for example, have moved Bader to somewhere like Kenley. At the same time Leigh-Mallory was not a team player; he was keen to make an impact in his own way.

These issues were also extensively considered in group 4, where *Sir Denis Crowley-Milling* took up cudgels on behalf of Leigh-Mallory, and the discussion moved on to the question of Dowding's dismissal. *Sir Denis* said that the story of Dowding being dismissed as a result of a plot by Sholto Douglas and Leigh-Mallory stemmed from Robert Wright's book (*Dowding and the Battle of Britain*). The person more responsible than either of these two was Sir John Salmond, who was pressing for his removal over night fighting. The real problem was not tactics, but personalities. Leigh-Mallory had taken over his Group in 1937, helped build up 12 and 13 Groups, and been promoted Air Vice-

Marshal in 1938. He then saw Park, who had been an Air Commodore SASO in Fighter Command, given 11 Group in the spring of 1940, when Leigh-Mallory was two to three years senior. Hence, the problem of personalities was built in.

Sebastian Cox asked *Sir Denis* if he accepted the implication from *Dr Orange*'s talk that Leigh-Mallory did not listen. "No," replied *Sir Denis*. "If he had not listened to Douglas Bader, there would have been no Big Wing. We all have our faults, but I thought that Leigh-Mallory was seriously maligned this morning. We came back from France badly demoralized. My Flight Commander had had a nervous breakdown, and my Squadron Commander was court-martialled. We flew into Coltishall from France and entered the dispersal hut, and there was the first AVM that I, a very new Pilot Officer, had ever seen in my life. We sat down and Leigh-Mallory talked to us about the forthcoming battle."

Wg Cdr Langley took the question further. Leigh-Mallory had had a bad press not only in terms of the Battle of Britain but also over his later career, so how was it that he not only maintained his position, but actually furthered it, until he was tragically killed? *Sebastian Cox*, having observed that Portal was unlikely to have allowed Leigh-Mallory to be put into high command positions if he was not up to the job, said that he had an unfortunate tendency to be somewhat pompous, and the Americans did not take to that. He did not have the happy facility, possessed by Tedder and others, for getting on well with the Americans, and that, in a coalition war as the junior partner, was a serious handicap. That was part of the reason that he found himself increasingly bypassed in his position as C-in-C Allied Expeditionary Air Force. It was probably an unworkable command structure in any case, but it was certainly unworkable without goodwill between the Allies. Tedder had the goodwill and trust of the Americans, as did Coningham, but Leigh-Mallory did not. Leigh-Mallory did, however, have qualities which ought, in justice to him, to be put on record. He was one of the first to call for the development of fighter-bombers. He was an Army co-operation expert, so his appointment to AEAF was entirely sensible, and furthermore the inter-Service aspect of his appointment should not be forgotten — he was perceived as sympathetic by the British Army, an important consideration. He was also an expert in the handling of large numbers of aircraft, and in planning for their use offensively.

Wg Cdr Langley then asked whether Leigh-Mallory's role in the shabby treatment accorded to Park and Dowding after the Battle of Britain had also had its effect, and *Sir Denis Crowley-Milling* took the opportunity to refer to the report on wing operations submitted by Leigh-Mallory on 17 September. Park also sent a report at the same time, and they were forwarded to the Air Ministry within a couple of days of each other. Why Dowding never retained these reports, and why he did not have a meeting at Fighter Command to discuss tactics, *Sir Denis* did not know, but Dowding sent them to the Air Ministry supporting both his Group commanders. It was therefore not surprising that the meeting of 17 October was called by the Air Ministry, because Dowding had put the ball in their court. He thought it unfair, therefore, to say that Leigh-Mallory was responsible, through the wing affair, for their removal. Sholto Douglas might be a different matter; *Sebastian Cox* could perhaps comment on this.

This was an immensely complicated subject, said *Cox*, far more complicated than most people thought, and involving many different factors. There was the fact, unpalatable to some, that Dowding was not a good co-operator. At times he seemed to be conducting two wars: one against the Germans, and one with the Air Staff and the Ministry. In fact the Air Ministry were very supportive of Fighter Command and everything that it did.

There were several myths perpetrated — one being that Dowding single-handedly dissuaded the Cabinet from sending more fighters to France. In fact, equal (if not greater) credit belonged to Newall. Dowding had undoubtedly urged Newall to take such a line in Cabinet, but if Newall (who as CAS had to take a wider strategic view than the more parochial concerns of a C-in-C) had felt that fighters should go to France, then Dowding would not have been present at the Cabinet meeting. He was, in effect, there to support Newall's presentation, not *vice versa*.

A further myth was that two Air Vice-Marshals, Douglas and Leigh-Mallory, had somehow manoeuvred an Air Chief Marshal out of his post by conducting a whispering campaign against him. Air Vice-Marshals might be powerful figures, but not that powerful, and such a suggestion did not say much for the senior figures on the Air Staff, such as Portal and Sir Wilfrid Freeman. Both were shrewd judges of character and highly intelligent men. They would not have countenanced the removal of a C-in-C merely on the say-so of two more junior and undoubtedly ambitious officers, particularly as the faults and ambitions of Leigh-Mallory and Douglas were as plain to them as the faults of Dowding. The latter, not the former, were the key.

Dowding was removed from his post for several reasons. One was the problem of night air defence, which he was thought not to be grasping with sufficient energy. Another was the dangerous deterioration in relations between the two Group commanders, which again Dowding had not grasped. It was important to make a distinction here between Air Staff concern over the latter and the actual causes of the dispute between 11 and 12 Groups; the former was viewed more seriously than the latter. The visit to Duxford, which had been mentioned in the morning, was about that deterioration, and the memo that Balfour wrote on his return from Duxford only mentioned tactics in passing; it was fundamentally about the diabolical relations between the two Group commanders, which were jeopardizing operational efficiency. Douglas then wrote to Dowding, pointing this out and saying that it was for Dowding to sort it out. It should never have been necessary for the Deputy Chief of the Air Staff to write to an operational commander telling him to sort out a disagreement between two of his subordinates.

With regard to night air defence, it was implied that Sir John Salmond's political manoeuvrings were merely those of a disgruntled retired officer. This was not so. Salmond actually held a post within the Ministry of Aircraft Production, and he had been asked by his minister, Beaverbrook, to look into night air defence problems, because the latter was concerned at the increasing effectiveness of night attacks on the aircraft industry. Salmond's remit was later extended, by agreement with the Air Ministry, to include the RAF. It was therefore quite legitimate for Salmond to bring his concerns to the attention of those at the highest level. His concern was with the fate of his country, and it was right and acceptable that he should make his strongly-held views known, if he believed — as he plainly did — that we were in danger of losing the night battle because of command failures.

Denis Richards referred to the same issues in group 1. He was quite clear that Dowding should have been alert to this difference of opinion, because Park — who was really rather indiscreet — was saying to his controllers: "We are getting excellent co-operation from 10 Group, but you can't rely on the same from 12 Group, so you must address your requests not to 12 Group but to Fighter Command". *Richards* had interviewed Dowding and

Sholto Douglas, but not Leigh-Mallory, and had stayed with Park in Malta. It was ridiculous to present Douglas as just a schemer; he might have been a bit of that, but he was a very clever man, and — if one had been interviewing Dowding and Douglas for a big job — one would have put one's money on Douglas. He was a very clever fellow and a good commander, though he lost his way a bit after the war. He might have had ambitions, but he was basically concerned with the problem of night defence. This Big Wing affair had been blown up out of all proportion. Dowding really went, as *Dr Orange* said, because of what was happening to British cities. While Dowding was working on the right lines — AI, GCI, and so on — the staff wanted other ideas tried too. These ideas were probably not much good, but Dowding was such a difficult chap to deal with that he was finally pushed aside.

John Ray, the author of a thesis on the subject, observed that Dowding really went because he lost political support. He lost that of Beaverbrook, who — even though a friend and great admirer of Dowding — was scared stiff about the bombing of his factories. Churchill, who thought so much of Dowding as late as August, also realized that he had got to go; Churchill chaired the Cabinet Sub-Committee on Night Air Defence and realized what a cussed man Dowding could be. Dowding's copy of the Salmond Committee report was also revealing; he had marked the paragraphs with a tick if he agreed with them, a question mark if he wasn't sure, and a cross if he disagreed. Of the eighteen paragraphs, seventeen were marked: three with ticks, five with question marks, and nine with crosses. It was Dowding's idea that "I'm right, and everyone else is wrong".

Denis Richards, having mentioned that both Beaverbrook and Churchill tried to find other employment for him, asked how far Dowding was really responsible for the system. It was normally accepted that when he was at the Air Ministry as Air Member for Supply and Research from 1930 onwards he approved the specifications for the Hurricane and the Spitfire, but other things were rarely mentioned. Watson-Watt, in his book about radar, did not even list Dowding amongst the four most helpful people in the RAF who hurried it on. His No. 1 helpful was Sholto Douglas, and Freeman and Newall also rated well, but Dowding was well down the list — presumably because he was a cautious man who wouldn't accept anything until it was proved in black and white. Park told *Richards* that when the RDF chain was established Dowding would still rely on standing patrols, and it wasn't until he (Park) actually connected the stations up with Fighter Command headquarters in the course of an exercise, and Dowding actually saw it working, that he said that this could become part of the system. He wasn't a chap who was rushing out in the forefront of technology.

As for Park, he went in December, a month after Dowding. They seemed to have been considered separately. Park was probably regarded as very tired by that time, having been in command since April — this being a very intense period. He wasn't wasted in Flying Training and, of course, was very soon picked up by Portal, who maintained an intense belief in Park's abilities right through until about 1945.

Sir Christopher Foxley-Norris said how fascinated he was, having become a commander many years later, that most of the senior RAF commanders never went on a station. Portal never visited one operational station in four years as CAS; Bomber Harris only went to one, and that was for the Dams raid; and Dowding never went to stations during the Battle. Commanders of our generation would consider it absolutely of the essence. The Germans did it; Kesselring visited all the time.

AVM Hunter mentioned the contrast with Park, and *Denis Richards* referred to his flamboyance; he flew around in his Hurricane in his white flying suits and was a very noticeable figure arriving on units. Leigh-Mallory, for whom no one had a good word, was also very popular with his pilots; he was a good talker, too, and they thought a lot of him, so it was not one-sided. Portal, incidentally, did visit his squadrons when he was C-in-C Bomber Command, but he didn't visit anywhere as CAS. Dowding went to quite a lot of night interceptions during the Battle.

Wg Cdr Ross, observing that today's RAF was used to being fairly anonymous, both in the press and the public eye, asked how the wartime commanders were seen by the public and the press, and what the press reaction was to their downfall. *Denis Richards* observed that it had very little impact. *Dr Orange* had said that the Air Ministry had suppressed the name of Dowding in the first accounts. It was not suppressed, said Richards. The story was written up on the basis of blanket instructions from the Department of Public Relations, which was determined not to create personal heroes. In World War I a lot of ill-feeling had been caused by blowing up the reputations of certain "aces", when these chaps had done no more than others in their squadrons, so when World War II started the view was that we shouldn't personalize. There was trouble in France with a New Zealander named Cobber Kane, because the press (Noel Knights, of the *Daily Mail*) got hold of his story and blew it up. This caused some ill-feeling amongst the rest, so they decided to operate under this limitation. In that pamphlet, therefore, no individual was mentioned on the British side, and only Göring, he thought, on the German. There was no desire to do down Dowding, but the man who wrote it (who was a colleague of *Richards*) was told to leave out personalities. So it was not a conspiracy.

The discussion then switched to the senior German commanders, and *Brig-Gen Strzebniok* expressed the view that Kesselring, Sperrle and Stumpff were all extremely competent commanders. All had a service background, either in the Imperial Flying Service in World War I or in the Army, and all had been with the Luftwaffe from its inception. They were extremely competent, and *Strzebniok* did not think that they could be criticized at all. The real difference between the German and British commanders was that Göring was a hopeless disaster as C-in-C, whereas — whatever might be said about Dowding — he was pretty competent.

Herr Jurgenmeyer, observing that the Germans did not make a special study of their commanders' performance, agreed with this assessment of Kesselring, Stumpff and Sperrle, adding that Göring had in former times been a very good pilot. However, he later rose to a level that was a little too much for him. *Denis Richards* took this point further: Göring was not only Air Minister, but also Hitler's deputy, President of Prussia, head of the Gestapo, and so on; he had his finger in too many pies. There were also his own sybaritic tendencies: for instance, in July, when the Luftwaffe was trying to improvise an attack against Britain, he had a complete fortnight in Paris buying works of art. He was also one of the people involved in making peace initiatives. Hitler, of course, was also prepared to make peace on his own terms, but these collapsed because the result would have been German hegemony over Europe. These views of Göring were endorsed elsewhere, with a German Colonel mentioning that newsreels portrayed him as a charismatic figure, meeting his men at the front, yet he was often absent and uninterested in the Battle at a time when the Luftwaffe needed decisions from him.

In group 3 *Dr Boog* took a slightly different view of the

background of the Luftwaffe's operational commanders. The absence of an air force between the end of World War I and the early 1930s had hindered the development of an understanding of how to manage large formations, and this accounted for much of the difference between Luftwaffe and RAF leadership, and for some of the mistakes made. About the less senior German commanders little was said, though *Denis Richards* made specific reference to good men like Molders. He also mentioned the moment in the Battle when Göring said his fighter commanders were too old, and shunted about six of them — a most unfair move, though it did advance the career of Galland. On the whole, *Richards* thought the younger German commanders were very good.

Richards also commented on Saul and Brand, Dowding's other AOCs, neither of whom had received much mention elsewhere. In his opinion, they were both excellent, though Saul was more or less out of it except for intercepting the odd aircraft and operating against shipping — apart, of course, from coping with the big day on 15 August, when the first intimation that there would be a big raid on the north of England came from radar (not from an *Enigma* source, or anything like that), and it was all handled perfectly. So Saul was a very competent commander, as was Brand.

At the next level, *Richards* went on, there were some quite outstanding station commanders, who were a great source of inspiration to squadron commanders on their stations, in particular Victor Beamish. For his recent book *Richards* had sent out something like 550 questionnaires to surviving Battle of Britain pilots and had received answers from about 260, which was pretty good. It was surprising how many of them mentioned Victor Beamish, though, of course, there were others — such as Atcherley and Vincent, who took off from Northolt and turned back a whole raid. At the squadron level, many of the commanders were extremely good, but others were not good at all, and the pilots were constantly covering up for them. One of the troubles here was the posting system; chaps were being killed off and replaced by posting someone from, say, the Air Ministry who had the right rank and seniority but no recent experience. This was a very real deficiency. He had received a letter from one pilot who was out in France when his CO was killed, followed by his flight commander. The other flight commander took over the squadron and then told this chap, a sergeant, that he was the new flight commander. He replied that he couldn't be, because there were Flight Lieutenants on the squadron, but was told to get on with it. Then the new CO was killed, and this chap took over, having gone from NCO pilot to CO in about a week. He was, of course, first-class.

Let the last word on this subject rest with *Sir Kenneth Cross*, who had written down the names of some of the squadron commanders he knew in the Battle of Britain: men like Sailor Malan, Rodney Wilkinson, Tommy Thomson and Douglas Bader (whose greatest value was to inspire his men because he was frightened of nothing). As Sir Kenneth said, they were all totally different.

E. THE STRATEGY

British strategy during the Battle generated little discussion, for there was no dispute that the twin objectives of containing the German onslaught and achieving air superiority over the Channel had been unswervingly followed. The German failure to decide on a campaign strategy and adhere to it occasioned most comment, a point made by *Gp Capt Haslam*, when he observed: "one is struck by the lack of strategic co-ordination on the German side. The High Command never really selected their aim, and vacillated between one target system and another."

ACM Sir John Aiken pursued the same theme, adding that the Luftwaffe aim "should have been air superiority over south-eastern England", and *Derek Wood* observed that target policy seemed to change constantly, and that there was no detectable bombing policy. He elaborated, saying: "The Luftwaffe arrived on the French coast much more quickly than it had expected, and had nothing prepared. In France and Belgium one good strike was enough to knock out an airfield. We kept our airfields going, but German intelligence just wrote them out after one attack."

There was some airing of the political background to this situation. *Gp Capt. Madelin* took the view that the German failure may have arisen because: "Feeling on the Continent was that Britain was in effect defeated, and some sort of accommodation was needed, so that we could be brought to the negotiating table. Hitler was disappointed that we would not come to terms, and so had to follow through with the invasion plan."

Edward Thomas reinforced this point: "This is why Hitler was so very hesitant. He was very uncertain about whether an invasion would ever come off. More than anything else, he hoped political forces would rise to the surface in this country and make common cause with him against Russia. Britain was the cradle of capitalism, with a ruling class with values that were anathema to Communism, and there were, after all, some quite high figures who sympathized with Hitler. However, by the end of July his 'peace offensive' had collapsed, and that is when he issued his first instructions for preparing an invasion. He was certainly very uncertain of the prospects for a successful invasion, and I can never be sure in my own mind that he was not just trying to exert pressure — the biggest form of pressure, of course, being the Battle of Britain. If he could have worn down the RAF, he must have expected that the political profile would alter, and that he would perhaps obtain his objectives without having to invade."

Turning to German strategy during the Battle, *AVM Mason* considered that here were two basic weaknesses: the failure to concentrate on any one target system and, although German attacks were eroding Fighter Command's strength, the failure to obtain strategic returns for these efforts. He felt that: "7 September was the watershed, for, by taking the pressure off the fighter bases, the Luftwaffe made the task of the defence easier, allowing concentration against easily identified raids without significant diversions."

It had been claimed that the Luftwaffe did achieve its primary aim of winning air superiority over the Channel, said *Gordon Browne*, but *AVM Bird-Wilson* disputed this, for its object was to penetrate deeper and beat the RAF, which it failed to do. *Browne* then quoted Kenneth Macksey's argument that, having achieved a degree of air superiority over the landing areas, the Germans might have succeeded, had they tried to invade in September. *Sir Kenneth Cross* doubted this because, as Allied experience in Italy and Sicily later showed, one needed more than just superiority over the landing areas; one needed air supremacy.

In the view of *Dr Boog*, "The Luftwaffe lacked a clear concept of what air war lay ahead. German doctrine contained in Air Force Manual 16, though good in broad theory, made virtually no reference to air superiority. Thinking was still too much influenced by Douhet and the idea of enemy air power being destroyed on the ground." He agreed, however, that the

Luftwaffe had failed to observe the principle of selection and maintenance of the aim.

What, then, the Luftwaffe's policy should have been in order to win the Battle was raised by *Sir Denis Smallwood*, and it was *Derek Wood*'s view that it should have concentrated on airfields, pounding those within reach of the Me 109s and concentrating especially on the Sector stations; south-east England would then have been virtually untenable.

Following the same theme, *Air Cdre Probert* expressed the view that the Luftwaffe had not planned or trained for the Battle but, although getting a bloody nose at the hands of the RAF at Dunkirk, was supremely confident about what lay ahead. One of the students at the Führungsakademie commented: "The Germans' view of the Battle was different from the British, for they looked at it in 'operative' terms. The Germans saw their ultimate enemy as Russia . . . and believed that Britain could be forced into suing for peace." Agreeing, *Colonel Schulte-Sasse* said that Hitler's long-term strategy was to defeat Russia and, "although Britain remained undefeated, she was practically powerless. The German Navy was quite content to stand back and let the Luftwaffe try to win air superiority over the Channel. Certainly, however, it was a strategic requirement, not just an operational one, to take out Great Britain." He later reinforced the point by stating: "*Mein Kampf* shows that it was always Hitler's long-term aim to attack Russia. Victory over France surprised him in its scope, and the Battle of Britain had to be improvised. Hitler wanted the Low Countries, but he did not want the destruction of the British Empire."

Air Cdre Probert referred to the difference between German and British definitions of strategy, but went on to say: "Taking out Great Britain should have been part of the Germans' overall strategy. The Germans were afraid of war on two fronts — they had to safeguard their rear against Russia. The result of the Battle of Britain was therefore clearly a strategic defeat for the Germans, which led to their eventual defeat." Turning to the respective higher command structures, he referred to *Dr Boog*'s suggestion that the German structure was diffuse and incompetent. While he felt that *Dr Orange* had exaggerated the RAF's shortcomings, since its structure did at least provide links between the technical, intelligence, research and operational fields, and the means of rapid consultation were available, he observed that Martini's signals organization, for example, was ignored by the German High Command; there was no machinery for such organizations to be brought into consultation, so they lacked status, power and authority. *Dr Boog* endorsed this view, for he felt that essential links were not built into the Luftwaffe system; to some extent Göring could have provided the necessary cohesion but failed to do so. *Gp Capt Haslam* commented on the lack of tri-Service co-operation and recalled a conversation, long after the war, with Admiral Ruge, who had said: "The Wehrmacht would never have crossed the Channel; the German soldier is sick if he crosses the Rhine."

Gp Capt Madelin said it was well known that the invasion plan was not popular with the German Navy, Admiral Raeder believing that any invasion would be a non-starter without full air control of the Channel area. However, once the RAF was neutralized, it would become a seriously intended plan. The lack of co-ordination was commented on by *Denis Richards*: "Göring was very proud of being the head of the Luftwaffe, and he told Hitler he could do the job at Dunkirk — which he failed to do. I'm sure he felt he could the job in England, that he could produce a situation which the Germans would know would make for an easy occupying force. One of the most remarkable things about all this is that when the Germans got an invasion plan finally agreed between the Navy and the Army after great dispute, the Air Force hardly came into it; there was absolutely no co-ordination on the invasion between the Luftwaffe and the other two Services." Asked whether he, too, felt that this was because Göring was not fulfilling his role as head of the Luftwaffe, *Richards* replied: "No, not really. Where I think the real deficiency lay was that the Germans had no proper equivalent of the Chiefs of Staff, or the Combined Chiefs of Staff Committees, able to take a real overview of the war. The OKW was not the equivalent of the British COS Committee, with the Prime Minister as Minister of Defence."

F. WRITING THE HISTORY

(EDITORIAL NOTE: *This Digest concludes with a statement made by Cecil James, who worked on the original RAF Narrative of the Battle:*

The Air Historical Branch of the Air Ministry understandably gave priority to producing a narrative of the Battle of Britain, including an account of the development of the Fighter Command system of control before the war and in the first months of the war. The Command, Group and other records were assembled at the National Library of Wales in Aberystwyth and were the basis of a day-to-day detailed narrative as seen from the British side. The record enabled the historian to paint a picture of each day's activity, usually beginning with a perceived build-up of Luftwaffe activity over northern France, followed by movement over the Channel towards the English coast. How the fighter controllers reacted, what squadrons were scrambled and at what times, and the results of combat, including damage to airfields, radar stations and other targets — relevant records were available on all these aspects of the Battle. The resultant narrative, exceedingly detailed, has been useful to subsequent historians writing more digestible accounts of the Battle. It was, however, clear from the start of the historical analysis that RAF claims of German losses were excessive (as were German claims of RAF losses).

The claims were genuine, but, by the nature of the Battle, it was not surprising that one aircraft could be reported as destroyed or damaged by more than one pilot; other aircraft, thought to have been destroyed, could have limped back to France. There was no policy of inflating claims to hearten the general public, and the Air Historical Branch was required to discover, if it could, what the actual German losses were. This was impossible to do from British records (e.g., of aircraft wrecks and prisoners captured), and a small task force, led by a Squadron Leader from Air Intelligence, was dispatched to Germany in the spring of 1945 to find the relevant German records. These were discovered in the office of the Luftwaffe Quartermaster-General, who had to produce aircraft to replace those lost: an invaluable record, covering most of the war, and complete for the summer of 1940. No better documents have been discovered, and the German losses they record are now accepted by historians as reliable. A copy is lodged in the Imperial War Museum.

10. Lessons for Today

Air Chief Marshal Sir Michael Knight

Even before such a day as this, it was always going to be difficult to say anything new about the Battle of Britain. Indeed, so much has been researched, written, documented and filmed from all possible standpoints, that there can, in truth, have been only the odd gap, the occasional reminiscence, the last "recollection in tranquillity", to complete the picture. And those last pieces of the jigsaw have, I am sure, been duly slotted into position during the course of the day. Now I am called upon to speak for just twenty minutes, "without hesitation, repetition or deviation", before an audience which contains about as much experience of the Battle — direct and indirect — as could now be collected together anywhere in the world. A tall order indeed, which it takes either bravery or foolhardiness to accept. You will be the judges.

I have been specifically asked for a view on the significance of the Battle to the modern Royal Air Force, and I appear before you — although a fully paid-up member of the RAF Historical Society — not as a historian. However, I am with Kirkegaard in believing that "whereas life has to be lived forwards, it can only be understood backwards". Anyway, do I not stand on a stage which has echoed, for nearly thirty years, to the sounds of cheery, young, "specially selected", glad-to-be-here, middle-ranking officers of the Royal Air Force (and some of its sister Services) busily engaged in fighting again that stirring Battle of Summer 1940 in the annual exercise "See Adler"? Incidentally, I'm still not sure quite why it had that title: but then I wasn't a very good student here, at the best of times.

"The Pink" of that famous exercise would (I recall) have us etch in the forefront of our respective minds that the Battle proved, beyond peradventure, the importance of that first of all the ten principles of war — viz. "selection and maintenance of the aim". Certainly it would seem unarguable that, between them, Hitler and his corpulent Reichsmarschall failed to heed that principle on both counts. And that was, I suppose, a lesson well learned by those who were to practise such things in the years that followed.

But surely there is more to it than that? Indeed there is, given a Battle which has been described as "one of the most significant . . . in history" — the outcome of which "had a profound effect on the future of the civilized world". That was, of course, the view of "the two Dereks" — Wood and Dempster — in their admirable "bible" of the Battle, *The Narrow Margin*. But their words have been echoed by others. Telford Taylor, examining the Battle in the context of Nazi Germany's overall performance that fateful year, characterized Hitler's failure as, in the strategic sense, "the War's turning point" — "a crucial episode in the modern history of Mankind". Slightly more restrained (but he would be, wouldn't he?), Dr Karl Klee (in his *Decisive Battles of World War II — The German View*) is quoted by John Terraine as follows:

> *The invasion and subjugation of Britain was made to depend on victory in that battle; and its outcome, therefore, materially influenced both the further course and the fate of the War as a whole.*

I would have thought that to be, if anything, somewhat understating the case, but let us leave it to others to speculate on the likely outcome had the Battle been lost; had "Operation Sealion" been, in consequence, attempted; and had it, after however sturdy a resistance, succeeded. The immediate future courses of Germany and Japan, the Soviet Union, the United States and many other nations would have been very different from what they were. And who could divine the consequences of all that?

For now, let us concentrate on some of the more parochial — but, in truth, more tangible — consequences of a battle which was well and truly won; and not (as Wood and Dempster point out) "in the period from July to October 1940 alone. The outcome was the culmination of the preparation, good judgment and error, made in the preceding seven years."

Now that (as they freely admit) is to take nothing from the gallantry, on both sides, of those who fought; nor to deny the immeasurable efforts of very many other "Players" — particularly in the British team:

— The ground crews, who worked every hour that God sent — often enough, at very real personal risk — to keep Fighter Command in the air;
— The station personnel — men and women — at fighter airfields who performed heroically in direct support of the front-line;
— Those who so quickly repaired damaged airfields and their facilities;
— The controllers and their assistants, on whose cool skills success in Battle so much depended;
— Those working in the civilian repair organization, achieving near miracles in producing no less than 35% of the aircraft issued to Fighter Command during the Battle;
— Those (civilians again) who assembled the other 65% — more than a thousand new fighters produced between April and June 1940 and, astonishingly, nearly 500 a month during the Battle itself — one very powerful manifestation of that famous "Dunkirk Spirit";
— The men and women of the often unfairly criticized Post Office who, with help (as we have heard) from industry, achieved miracles of their own by the speed and secrecy of installation and by the daily practice of recovery of land-lines, teleprinter links and other equipments vital to the control of the Battle;
— And, whilst talking of civilians, let us not forget those who suffered in the bombing of towns and cities, as Hitler's forces were directed away from a potentially winning strategy. It may not have been generally realized, at the time, that their prolonged period of trial was in fact a consequence of Nazi Germany's first major defeat.
— There were the wives of some (and the families of most) of those in the front line, who daily suffered agonies of apprehension and, all too often, of grief in their loss;
— And finally, of course, there were the commanders, who bore the great weight of responsibility for directing their very limited resources over perhaps the most difficult and danger-ous three months of World War II. From station level up to the very highest in the Command, theirs was an exceptional example of our having the right men in the right place at the right time: something which, however hard we try in peace-

time, can neither be guaranteed nor — more significantly — proved until conflict is engaged.

Today we have rehearsed again some of those old arguments about who was right — and whether or not there were better or easier ways to win the Battle of Britain. I would only say that, as in so many other activities, "a win is a win". And almost everything in my own reading of the Battle suggests that, in terms of overall achievement, Dowding and Park deserve almost unstinted praise. It seems to me incredible that, still at a time of real danger, the Service could afford itself the luxury of debate — let alone, recrimination — over a battle which had not only been clearly won but which, in scope and kind, was unlikely ever to be repeated. Lessons were, of course, there to be learned — and so they should have been. But there is, for me, something almost unhealthy in the way in which that was done; and in the distinctly underwhelming vote of confidence in the two men on whom the overall direction of the Battle had rested. It was not a great morale-booster for those they had led, either: but that's another story.

What is, I believe, incontrovertible is that Dowding's work during the decade which culminated in the Battle of Britain was totally vindicated — and on three counts. As Air Member for Supply and Research (oh, how times, and jobs, change!), his was the well-placed hand which helped the Hurricane and Spitfire into service; and, as the first Commander-in-Chief of Fighter Command, his was the responsibility for developing the famous "system", for preparing his forces for war and — something granted to few leaders — for then proving his own creation in battle. At least the Almighty allowed him that, even if some of his own colleagues and subordinates were unable to share that magnanimity.

Now I am supposed to be here to relate the events of 1940 to the Air Force of today. In fact, it would be stretching a few points to do that too directly — or in too great detail. Times have, indeed, changed as dramatically for air power in the fifty years since the Battle of Britain, as they had in the fifty that preceded it. But there are several general and telling features of the Battle that have not been lost on successive generations of the Royal Air Force — and, indeed, air forces the world over.

Firstly: the absolute necessity for adequate and timely preparation for any major national activity — and, certainly, for war. I'll say more of that later.

Secondly: the need for armed services as a whole (but I believe it to apply absolutely to air forces) to stay always at the very sharp end of technology. The Royal Air Force was, belatedly, allowed to do that in the frantic run-up to World War II. It was, of course, almost *too* late, though that's a lesson more for politicians than for military men. But had there been no Hurricane, no Spitfire, no Merlin, no Browning; had a small number of very determined people not argued consistently (and, in the end, successfully) for eight guns per fighter, or for the development of radar — to take just two obvious examples; had scientists and operators not been able to work closely together on such projects (which, as my friend Professor R. V. Jones has reminded us, was one of the very important lessons of the War — not, specifically, of the Battle of Britain); had there been no careful stitching together of a viable system of aircraft and their crews, airfields and their supporting infrastructure, radar, static defences, sectors, ops rooms and communications; had all this not come about, then the Battle of Britain would, in all probability, have been lost — however great the individual efforts of that most gallant band of aircrew: "the gayest company who ever fired a gun in anger". (How infuriating it is that that very useful little adjective has been hijacked for other purposes!).

So — as Horace and others have reminded us over the years — preparation for war is the continuing adjunct of peace; and, if the peace be broken, remains the soundest guarantee of victory. That may not always be a popular policy; it was not so in the years up to 1938, and I suspect it will become steadily less popular in the years immediately ahead of us. But, in truth, we have enough evidence in history of the consequences of inadequate preparation to convince the majority in our electorates. What we must continue to have — as, fortunately, we have long had in this country — are very professional military leaders who can, without overstating the case, convince politicians that electoral popularity is better founded on national security than on any other "social service". For without the first, there can be no guarantee of any other.

Next in the list of lessons learnt from the Battle — and, again, one that has been well covered in discussion today: from the German point of view (and, indeed, for all students of warfare) there is a very telling lesson in the overriding importance of effective intelligence — or, in the case of the Luftwaffe, the lack of it. In recent years, I have not been alone in conjuring up a sort of nightmare situation in which, through another great mis-calculation, we had been pitched into a World War III — and had lost. And at the post-war wash-up — in Heaven or the other place (come to think of it, it might have been tricky to get all the players together!) — we, the Allies, had come to the cold realiz-ation that we had, in fact, had all the intelligence information we needed to defeat the enemy, but it had just not got to the people who could use it: in other words, it was not *effective* intelligence.

In the period leading up to the outbreak of war, the Germans had had opportunity enough to unmask the mystery of British radar development. They failed to take it. In the weeks leading up to the Battle — indeed, throughout the Battle itself — they should certainly have come to realize the vital role that radar was playing and, equally important, the vulnerability of the radar stations. They should have properly assessed the value of close control of the RAF's limited number of fighters — responding not to every penetration of their airspace, not to raids which (by reason of height, geography, timing or reduced warning) could not be touched, but only to significant threats, against which they could hope to achieve success. And the Germans should have come to believe what they never did: that their own claims for the destruction of Fighter Command — in the air but also, particu-larly, on the ground — were grossly inflated; and that bombing an airfield does not put it permanently out of action — still less, take with it the squadrons based there.

Now I must home in on one or two of the lessons in applied leadership, which were not invented by Dowding, Park and Co., but very well exemplified by them. In pole position I would place teamwork — or so it seems to the non-participant, fifty years on. I have already touched on this and will say little more than that it remains at the very heart of any great endeavour and is still perhaps as successfully demonstrated in a fighting service — in peace or in war — as anywhere else. Without wishing in any way to compare the events of World War II with that very unusual enterprise in the South Atlantic eight years ago, I would say two things from the perspective of a Commander of that period. The first — I hope not too flippant — is that, tasked with the prep-aration, training and readiness of a significant element of British air power deployed to the combat area, but (quite properly) denied a role in "the action", I can understand something of what Leigh-Mallory felt in 1940. More importantly, we did for a short time in this country — and on a far less dramatic scale —

experience something of that sense of shared effort, determination and will to succeed which was such a vital element of the Battle we are discussing today. As far as 1982 went, there was a great deal of quiet satisfaction in having been a part of it.

My next lesson in applied leadership: the control of limited resources. No study of the Battle of Britain can fail to reveal the narrowness of that margin of victory; the several extremely close calls, when Fighter Command's very ability to survive was brought into question; and the markedly different ways in which the commanders of the two sides controlled their forces — particularly when the going got really tough. Of course, there could scarcely have been a greater contrast than that between the two "top men". There was Dowding, thinking, technically capable, sensitive but aloof, with the ability to engender great loyalty — even affection — in his men and to know their strengths and weaknesses while scarcely ever meeting them "in the field". A difficult achievement, that, and one that few of us might have had the self-confidence (or was it self-opinion?) to attempt. There are interesting parallels here (Harris for one) which may be more true of air commanders than of their colleagues in the other two combat environments — but that's the subject of another discussion (and may, anyway, suffer in the manner of all generalizations). Certainly it was not true of that other air commander: the aforementioned corpulent one. But I cannot honestly believe that it assisted the German cause that a man so clearly out of touch with the realities of air fighting in 1940 made his physical and psychological presence so very much felt on the other side of the Channel. Whatever his reputation for bravery in the very different environment of twenty and more years earlier, Göring was neither in knowledge, ability or temperament any match for Dowding. Sperrle and Kesselring were in a different league, and may well have been as good as their counterparts in England. For them, it may have been too harsh a judgment that emanated from Lieutenant Wolfgang Schenk — perhaps, significantly, a Bf 110 pilot — to the effect that "their leaders had taught them little, apart from dancing and drinking" (which attributes I do not, incidentally, decry absolutely but there is a place!).

Back to applied leadership. As several people in this room can attest from personal experience, one of the more unpleasant aspects of that extremely concentrated period of air combat was fatigue — a numbing, all-enveloping tiredness which could make simple activities difficult and mistakes an ever-present danger (to add to the many other present dangers). In Fighter Command those problems were very much more readily accepted and acted upon than seems to have been the case with Luftflotten 2 and 3. Unit rotation and rest-days undoubtedly helped on this side of the Channel — but seldom on the other. And that is an important lesson which has certainly been hoisted aboard by successive generations of Royal Air Force, and indeed other, commanders.

Of tactics, I will say little: the subject has been exhaustively covered today, as it has these fifty years past, by students and practitioners of air power. Certain it is that the Luftwaffe entered the Battle with a far greater tactical awareness than did their opponents in Fighter Command. But the latter very soon "caught on". Fighting and tactical formations, developed from those of the Luftwaffe, remain a feature of our training and, hence, of our operational capability. The speed and performance of modern fighter aircraft, together with technological advances which assist station-keeping, detection and mutual support, have inevitably brought into being some modifications to tactical capability — and, of course, even more to the practice of air defence. If nothing else, the impressive development of airborne intercept radars and the advent of the air-to-air missile, of AWACs and of advanced electronic warfare have seen to that. But, for the tactical formation seeking to maintain cohesion, flexibility and effectiveness, the essential elements of "stick, search, report" remain valid to this day.

As to training, I would like to think that we have held to Trenchard's maxim that quality must be the key. It was the quality of training that counted in 1940, because upon it quality could be built — certainly for a time. After that, there was an inevitable sense of "hand-to-mouth" about the provision of new pilots for Fighter Command. But if today we maintain the quality of our training, which we practise in the most realistic scenarios that are allowed by the constraints of peacetime, then the ability to build up in quantity has, sadly, been greatly reduced. Not only does it now take so long to train effective front-line aircrew that any likely European conflict over the past thirty-five years would have been over before the new recruit had even seen his operational mount, but we no longer have the backing of those in-practice reserves and auxiliaries on whom the maintenance of an effective air defence capability so greatly depended in 1940. I fear that my own current efforts, as a flying officer with No 4 Air

Experience Flight, would scarcely be a match for early commitment on a Tornado F3 in a shooting war. I reckon I should need at least a couple of days! But, as in so many other ways, the practice of air power has become too expensive a game for the part-timer — as has the maintenance of large inventories of combat aircraft by any nation.

Conscious of the pressure of time, let me move on quickly with the last three of my lessons learnt from the Battle of Britain. What that Battle clearly did, both at the time and in retrospect, was enormously to enhance the status, pride and morale of the Royal Air Force — the world's first independent air force, I would remind you, but one which had suffered some very hostile take-over bids during its first twenty years of existence. Of itself, the Battle did not divert those pressures; indeed, they have not yet been entirely released, and they may well build up again, as they tend to do whenever the squeeze on the nation's defence budget becomes really tight (I am confident, incidentally, that they can be resisted). But the Battle of Britain did prove to this country — and to the world — that warfare had graduated, once and for all, into "the third dimension"; and that the fate of nations could be decided by combat in which soldiers played precious little part. In a sense, of course, it was something of a "one off". As Wood and Dempster have written:

> It is unlikely that there will ever be a parallel to the Battle of Britain; where armies and navies, immobilized on either side of the Channel, watched a few thousand combatants meet in the air above.

Unrepeatable it may have been, but unarguable it certainly was. And I think that there will be very few wearing the light blue of the Royal Air Force in the years to come who will not be more than well aware of the importance of the Battle to the image of their Service. Incidentally, it also did a great deal for the morale of the nation at the time. I don't know how long that nation will wish to give thanksgiving for its deliverance in that annual commemoration at Westminster Abbey, but more than once in recent years an impressive number of "the great and good" have impressed on senior people in our Service the continuing importance of that very special event. We shall see.

There are, of course, some who see it as slightly ironic that a fighting service, developed on the precepts of offensive action and concentration of force, should be chiefly remembered for its success in a purely defensive battle. In response to that, may I first say that I refuse to denigrate, in any way, the efforts of all those engaged in the many other gallant and dangerous operations of the last war — perhaps, particularly, those of Bomber Command who, for so long, bore the brunt of action deep into enemy territory — and who have certainly been accorded, by some historians and others, far less than their due. That said, I am not myself unhappy that it is its performance in defence of the homeland that remains, in the eyes of most people, the lasting impression of my Service. After all, it's not a bad cause. And, as one who spent the greater part of his own front-line career in the "mud-moving" business, I was always conscious that we were training primarily to deter — and only if deterrence were ever to fail, then to fight a war. To my mind, deterrence and defence have always gone hand-in-hand; the one, like the other, showing the need for preparedness to fight — effectively, professionally and, of course, in timely fashion.

Which is why I take one last lesson from the great Battle that we have been considering today. However victory was gained in that Battle — and, indeed, in World War II itself — it was a very near-run thing. I think it was Group Captain Sir Hugh ("Cocky") Dundas who characterized it as being won by "a very large number of people, shooting down slightly more aircraft before they were shot down themselves". That victory was achieved says as much for the way in which Fighter Command had been prepared for battle — despite all the accompanying difficulties and frustrations — as it does about the undoubted gallantry and self-sacrifice of those who took part in it. But would it not have been better had there been no war in the first place? And, of course, I'm not talking of appeasement — let alone, of surrender — rather of deterrence.

And are there not now a few worrying "straws in the wind" as peace breaks out all over Europe and stalwart allies rush to cash in their so-called "peace dividends"? Genuine multilateral disarmament and the assurance of security at very much lower levels of military expenditure — by both sides: I'll buy that. But I would suggest that we really do need to pause, to see which way we're going (and, more importantly, which way the Soviet Union is going — and staying), before we lower our Transatlantic military guard too far, and write the obituary of an alliance which has stood us in such excellent stead these past forty-one years.

That, of course, is about twice the span of time between the last two European wars, each of which quickly assumed global status. I would be very happy to see that period extended by three, four or ten times. But I would feel a lot more comfortable were I to know that we were not threatened by unnecessary conflict which we had become militarily too weak to deter.

For me, the last and most important lesson of the Battle of Britain does not stem from the Battle itself, but from the events that preceded and precipitated it. In rereading some marvellously evocative literature during my researches for this short presentation, I was immediately struck by the very first paragraph of *The Narrow Margin*. It reads thus:

> The Treaty of Versailles, signed in June 1919, was intended to end German military aviation for ever. The Air Force was disbanded, and to the victorious allies were surrendered over 1,500 aircraft and 27,000 aircraft engines. Peace, like the Charleston, was in the air, and in England Geddes of the Anti-Waste Campaign was wielding his axe, reducing the Royal Air Force to a shadow of its former self.

It would be comforting, ladies and gentlemen, were that text to be placed on top of the briefing folders of all those Heads of State and Government meeting to sign another arms-control treaty, not twenty miles from Versailles, at the end of the fiftieth anniversary year of the Battle we have been recalling today.

11. Chairman's Closing Remarks

I cannot remember how often I have sat, not in this particular hall, but in this College, and after someone has said "I am not going to try and sum up" have then heard him go on for about twenty minutes trying to do so. You will be relieved to hear that I was only going to speak extremely briefly anyway, and since Air Marshal Knight has pinched four out of the five main points I was going to make, it will be even briefer.

The first point I want to stress particularly is that made by Dr Boog about the nature of the Luftwaffe. I think one of the reasons why I had difficulty in getting the right answer so many years ago was that we were baffled by numbers. We did not appreciate that the Luftwaffe was a tactical air force used to assist the advance of the Army, and indeed in Norway of the Navy. Fighter Command, by contrast, had just one purpose in life, namely to defend this country and gain air superiority, and that was one of the invisible assets that we had at the time.

Another point I must mention relates to the capabilities, the jealousies and the squabbles of the commanders. (Incidentally, if and when you all become very senior officers, you will not only have to win any war that the government may inflict on you, but you will also have to win the Whitehall battle as well. We have many potential enemies, but there are always the actual enemies in the Treasury and in the Government.) On the question of the personalities of the Battle of Britain commanders, I am not for a moment doubting anything that Dr Orange has told us, but it is a pity that the schedule of this exercise didn't give us the opportunity to hear as it were the other side. There is another side to the argument as between 11 Group and 12 Group and the Big Wing and Small Wing, but in any case I think the whole thing has been grossly exaggerated. In my opinion, to put it simply, it is a very good thing to put a large number of aircraft into one place to defend your country if you can. If you cannot do so it's because there isn't time to do it, and that was the difference between 12 Group and 11 Group.

There is one other little point which I recommend to you. We have heard today about the conduct of the Battle of Britain. Nobody has mentioned the invisible five weeks in between. The Battle of Britain was not only won partly because Dowding refused to send more fighters to France; it was also won because between June and July 10th, which is the official starting date of the Battle, he refused to commit unnecessary forces to targets that were less than valuable. There has been very little written about that, and I very much hope you will be able to appreciate the effect that that had on the actual outcome of the Battle.

I promised I was going to be brief and I am going to be brief, but I do want to mention the Battle of Britain Fighter Association, of which I have had the privilege of being Chairman for 12 years, in spite of a particularly undistinguished record during the actual Battle — when I put that to my colleagues they said "Oh get on with it, you can't make a cock of it again". In that context I would like to deny that the knighthood that the Federal Republic of Germany bestowed on me in later years was for services to the Luftwaffe in 1940.

I am going to finish by saying something rather un-British. We in the Battle of Britain Fighter Association are enormously proud of what happened in the Battle of Britain. I know we are supposed to be modest and shrinking and put it all down to luck and so on. It wasn't. The Battle of Britain was won because ordinary people on the ground and in the air behaved far above what could have been expected from them.

Biographical Notes

Air Chief Marshal Sir Christopher Foxley-Norris GCB DSO OBE

Air Chief Marshal Sir Christopher Foxley-Norris was born in 1917 and educated at Winchester College and Trinity College, Oxford, where he joined the University Air Squadron. On the outbreak of war he was called up and, following service with No 13 Squadron at Douai during the Battle of France, he volunteered for duty with Fighter Command. He joined No 3 Squadron at Turnhouse on 27 September, moving to No 615 Squadron at Northolt in November.

After surviving being shot down by an Me 109 on 26 February 1941, he was posted to CFS and from there he completed tours at 10 FTS and in Canada, where he instructed as part of the Commonwealth Air Training Scheme. Following tours with Ferry Command and Coastal Command, he was posted to the Middle East in 1944 to fly Beaufighters and took command of No 603 Squadron. He returned to the UK early in 1945 to command No 143 Squadron and was awarded the DSO soon after the end of the war.

Sir Christopher had a long and distinguished post-war RAF career, including command of the Oxford UAS, Directing Staff RAF Staff College, tours in FEAF and C-in-C RAF Germany. Sir Christopher retired from the RAF in April 1974, having been Chief of Personnel and Logistics on the Defence Staff for the last three years of his career.

Sir Christopher has been involved with the Cheshire Foundation since 1972 and has been Chairman of the Battle of Britain Fighter Association since 1978.

Air Chief Marshal Sir Michael Knight KCB AFC ADC BA DLitt FRAeS

Air Chief Marshal Sir Michael Knight was born in 1932 and educated at Leek High School and the University of Liverpool, where he flew with the University Air Squadron. He joined the RAF in 1954 and served in a variety of posts in Bomber and Transport Commands at home as well as in the Middle East and Near East Air Forces. His flying career included day-fighter ground attack, interdiction and strike/attack, tactical reconnaissance and survey, target marking, light- and medium-bomber, tactical and strategic transport and air-to-air refuelling.

He commanded No 32 Squadron in Akrotiri before attending 53 Staff Course at the RAF Staff College in 1954. After commanding the FEAF Canberra Strike Wing at Tengah from 1966 to 1969 he filled staff appointments at Strike Command and NATO HQ before taking command of RAF Laarbruch in 1973. Following a year at the RCDS he became Director of Operations (Air Support) in 1975 and SASO at Strike Command two years later. He was appointed AOC 1 Group in 1980 and AMSO in 1983. The last four years of his RAF career were spent in Brussels as the UK Military Representative to NATO.

A Fellow of the Royal Aeronautical Society, a member of the International Institute for Strategic Studies and a former Council member of the Royal United Services Institute for Defence Studies, Sir Michael is a frequent speaker and writer on defence and air power subjects.

Group Captain Thomas Percy Gleave CBE FRHistS RAF (Retd.)

Group Captain Gleave was born in 1908 and educated at Westminster High School and Liverpool Collegiate School. He learned to fly in 1927 and joined the RAF in 1930. Before the Second World War he served successfully with No 1 Squadron, CFS, 5 FTS, No 502 Squadron and at HQ Bomber Command.

In June 1940 he was given command of No 253 Squadron which flew Hurricanes from Kenley during the Battle of Britain and, during one remarkable sortie on 30 August, Group Captain Gleave shot down five Me 109s. The following day, however, he was shot down and severely burned during a large-scale air attack on Biggin Hill airfield.

He spent many months in the care of Sir Archibald McIndoe's team of plastic surgeons and became Vice-President of the Guinea Pig Club formed there in July 1941. He resumed operational flying in October 1941 and took command of RAF Manston. The following year he was posted to the Special Planning Staff and in 1943 he moved to the Allied Expeditionary

Air Force. Here he produced the Overlord Air Plan for the Normandy invasion. In September 1944 he became Head of Air Plans under General Eisenhower, a position which he held until the end of the war.

After the war, he held a variety of appointments until his retirement from the RAF in 1953. Since then he has been an Official Historian with the Cabinet Office Historical Section and has co-written six volumes of the Official History of the Second World War in the Mediterranean and the Middle East.

Dr Horst Boog

Dr Boog is a native of Leuna-Merseburg in Eastern Germany, where he suffered first-hand experience of Allied bombing. In 1944, at the age of sixteen, he underwent training as a glider pilot but then, instead of progressing on to the Heinkel 162 as had been intended, he was transferred to the Volksturm, an experience which he fortunately survived.

After the war he spent a short time as a translator and interpreter at Nuremberg and them went to the USA as an exchange student, one of the first German students to do so. Returning to Germany in 1950, he worked for the USAF in Germany on intelligence duties until 1964 and also studied part-time at the University of Heidelberg, where he obtained his PhD in 1965. Since then he has worked in the Military History Research Office in Freiburg as Senior Air Historian concentrating on the air aspects of the Second World War.

He has lectured extensively inside and outside Germany and has written a number of important works, including *German Air Force Leadership and Command, 1939–1945, The Strategic Air War and German Home Air Defence* and *The Attack on the Soviet Union.*

Dr Vincent Orange

Dr Orange was born in Shildon, County Durham, in 1935 and educated at St Mary's Grammar School, Darlington, and Hull University, where he gained a PhD. In 1962 he went to live in New Zealand and took up a post of lecturer in history at the University of Canterbury in Christchurch.

His varied career has included three years in the RAF and, as an actor, taking part in over seventy radio and stage plays; more recently he has regularly broadcast on a wide range of subjects. He has lectured many times to the New Zealand branches of the Royal Aeronautical Society (to which he was elected an Associate in 1980) and has published several articles on air battles of the Second World War.

His biography of Air Chief Marshal Sir Keith Park was published in 1984 and was followed by a biography of Wing Commander Johnny Checketts, a personal friend and one of New Zealand's best-known fighter pilots. His latest work is a biography of another New Zealand airman, Air Marshal Sir Arthur Coningham, which was published in 1990.

Mr John Alfred Terraine FRHistS

John Terraine was born in London in 1921 and educated at Stamford School and Keble College, Oxford. He joined the BBC in 1944 as a Recorded Programmes Assistant and did a variety of work including production of Radio Newsreel, programme assistant in the East European Service, and programme organizer of the Pacific and South African service. In 1963 he became associate producer and scriptwriter of the BBC Television series 'The Great War', for which he received the Screenwriters' Guild Documentary Award. He left the BBC in 1964 and scripted 'The Life and Times of Lord Mountbatten' for Thames Television in 1966. In 1974 he was scriptwriter and narrator of the BBC series 'The Mighty Continent'.

He is the author of many books including ten titles about the First World War, and is also the founding President of the Western Front Association. His other books include a biography of Lord Mountbatten, *The Mighty Continent* and his most recent work, *Business in Great Waters* which is a study of the U-boat campaigns in both World Wars. In 1985 he wrote *The Right of the Line*, a major new study of the RAF's part in the Second World War, and now a standard text on the subject.

In 1982, to mark his contribution to military history, John Terraine received the Chesney Gold Medal, the highest award of the Royal United Services Institute for Defence Studies. In 1987 he became a Fellow of the Royal Historical Society.

Mr Edward Eastaway Thomas OBE DCS

Edward Thomas studied German and music at university. He has had a long and varied career in military intelligence. During the

Second World War he joined the Naval Intelligence Division and served in Iceland and in the famous Hut 3 at Bletchley Park Manor as a Staff Officer (Intelligence), Home Fleet.

His career continued in strategic intelligence after the war in the Joint and Defence Intelligence Staffs. A student of the Imperial Defence Council, Mr Thomas has published translations of books by Helmut Schmidt and made a major contribution to the four-volume Official History of British Intelligence in the Second World War.

Mr Derek Harold Wood

Derek Wood was born in 1930 and educated at Chichester High School. He has been involved in aviation and defence publishing since 1948. His publishing career started with the journal *Aerosphere*, from which he moved on to become London Editor and later Managing Director of *Interavia*, a post which he held until 1983. He has also been air correspondent for a number of national and provincial newspapers, including *Liverpool Daily Post* (1952–60); *Westminster Press Provincial Newspapers* (1954–60) and the *Sunday Telegraph* (1961–68). In 1983 he became the founding editor of the new *Jane's Defence Weekly*, a journal which he pioneered through its first six years. In 1989 he became Head of Special Projects for Jane's Information Group.

Derek Wood is the author of many books, including *Project Cancelled*, *Attack Warning Red* (a history of the Royal Observer Corps, an organisation in which he served for over thirty years) and *Target England*. His best-known book is *The Narrow Margin*, which he wrote in 1961 in co-operation with Derek Dempster. The book was used as the basis for the 1968 film *The Battle of Britain* and is still considered to be one of the best works on the subject.

Royal Air Force Historical Society

The Royal Air Force has been in existence for more than seventy years; the study of its history is deepening, and continues to be the subject of published works of consequence. Fresh attention is being given to the strategic assumptions under which military air power was first created and which largely determined policy and operations in both World Wars, the inter-war period, and in the era of Cold War tension. Material dealing with post-war history is now becoming available for study under the thirty-year rule. These studies are important both to academic historians and to the present and future members of the RAF.

The RAF Historical Society was formed in 1986 to provide a focus for interest in the history of the RAF. It does so by providing a setting for lectures and seminars in which those interested in the history of the RAF have the opportunity to meet those who participated in the evolution and implementation of policy. The Society believes that these events make an important contribution to the permanent record.

The Society normally holds three lectures or seminars a year in or near London, with occasional events in other parts of the country. Transcripts of lectures and seminars are published in the Proceedings of the RAF Historical Society, which is a bi-annual publication provided free of charge to members. Individual membership is open to all with an interest in RAF history, whether or not they were in the Service. Although the Society has the approval of the Air Force Board, it is entirely self-financing.

Membership of the Society costs £15 per annum and further details may be obtained from the Membership Secretary, Commander Peter Montgomery, 26 Shirley Drive, Worthing, West Sussex BN14 9AY.

Acknowledgements

BRITISH AEROSPACE PLC

SMITHS INDUSTRIES PLC

AIRLIFE PUBLISHING LTD

The Royal Air Force Historical Society wishes to express its gratitude to British Aerospace, Smiths Industries and to Airlife Publishing Ltd for their generous assistance in the production of this special issue of its proceedings.